Savoring Eden

A JOURNEY OF PERSONAL DISCOVERY

Patricia Ann Woolfork
"Trishann"

Savoring Eden – A Journey of Personal Discovery
Copyright © 2018 by Patricia Ann Woolfork (aka "Trishann")

CBA Cares
An imprint of
CBA Publishing Services, LLC
cbapub.com
editor@cbapub.com

Artwork by Denise Jenious used with permission.
Jenious Crafty Creations on Amazon.com

All rights reserved. No part of this book may be reproduced or transmitted in any form or by any means including storage and retrieval systems–except in the case of brief quotations embodied in critical articles and reviews–without written permission of the author, except provided by the United States of America copyright law.

Disclaimer: The views, thoughts, and opinions expressed in the text belong solely to the author, and not necessarily to the author's editors and publisher of this work.

This book is for a mature audience and may not suitable for young readers; contains elements of violence, sex and sexual situations, as well as emotional, verbal, physical, and sexual abuse.

First Edition 2018

ISBN-13: 9781732474635

Savoring Eden

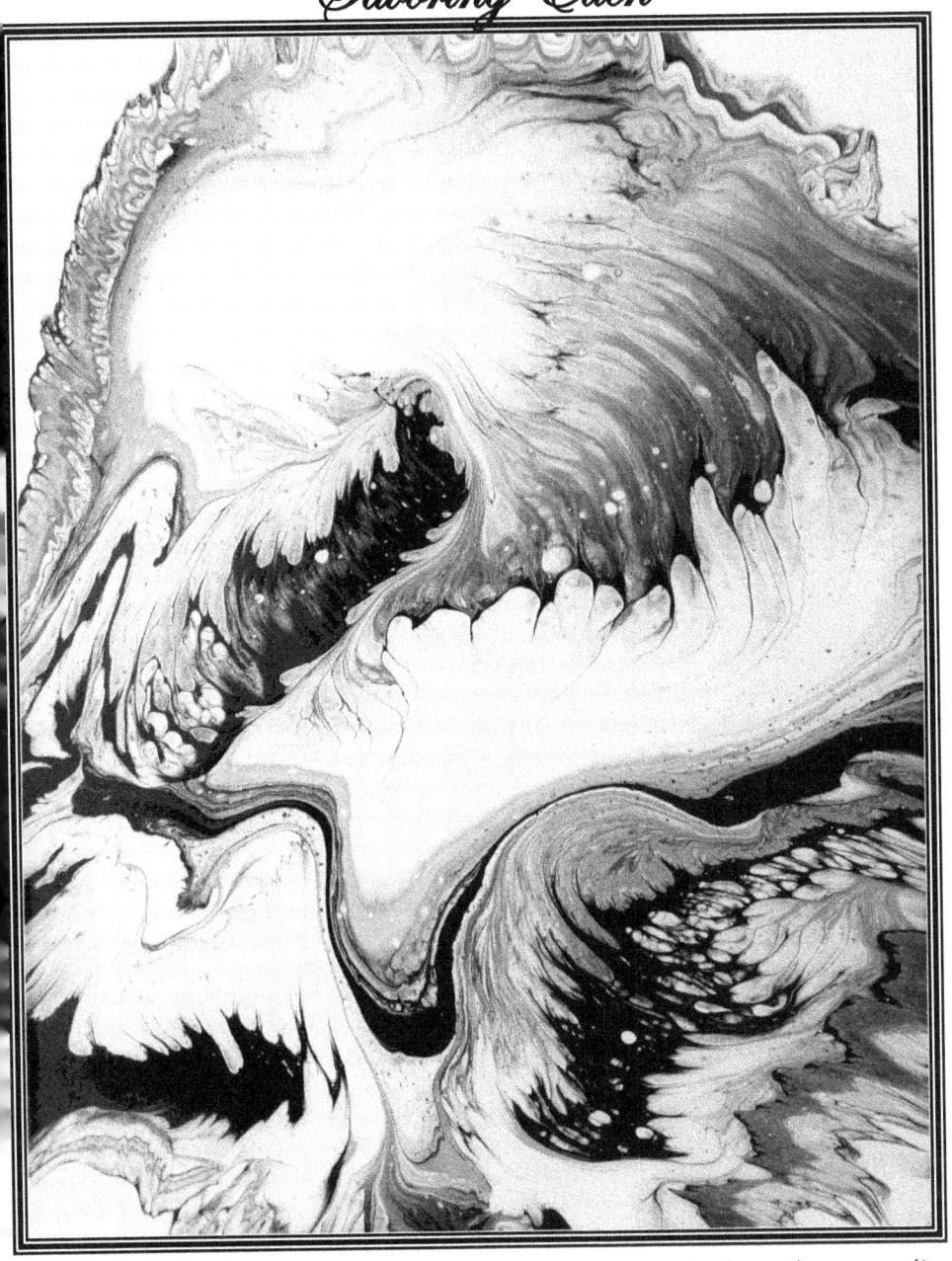

I chose this painting done by my friend, Denise Jenious, because it represented to me chaos and beauty. It called out to me because I could see myself within it. Can you find her?

Introduction

This book is a composite of my life's experiences in love, relationships, life and death, whether natural or symbolically. I have had the opportunity to use my words to express things that many of my past readers have told me they were unable to do for themselves. So I am happy to talk about a universal subject—the human condition. It's been wonderful to know that I have not been alone in some of these life experiences.

I have come a long way from the first printing of this book. I am stronger and happier, more enthusiastic and hopeful than ever. Perhaps that, too, comes with age. Better late than never! I can never turn my back on what led me to use this medium as an outlet, and I offer my love and compassion to others who have endured similar circumstances.

I would be remiss if I did not admit that even I have outgrown some of the sentiments in this book, but certainly someone is experiencing the joy and heartache in searching for love, finding and losing it. Nearly everyone experiences the need for love in their lives from time to time, and I'm happy to include mine in this collection.

This is not a book of love poems. It is a journey through the muck and mire of surviving each day to see another—looking for beauty in the ashes and finding it. I continue to write about the ups and downs of life and the beauty in nature and the growth and setbacks we all experience with relationships, raising children and health issues whether mental or physical.

I have found that the older I get, the more fearless I have become. I can say everything I have always wanted to say, tell my truth, take back my authority and my voice. I have found that when I share these thoughts and words, they comfort, encourage, empower, and motivate others to both find empathy and sympathy through shared experiences.

I take full responsibility for all the mistakes and bad decisions I have made. I bear no ill-will, throw no shade, nor wish to cause hurt feelings, or cast judgment with any of my writing in this book that may pertain to any interactions with family or others.

However, this is my story, my truth, as I perceive it or have in the past, when it was written, and it is now my time to tell it with all the passion that came with the experiences. So I ask for your forgiveness and understanding, in advance, if you feel privacy has been invaded, or that I have failed to give background and extenuating circumstances about anyone else's journey.

It is not my intention to shame or blame—just to give insight into the woman/mother whose inner demons have chased her since birth, and finally purge myself of them through this medium with the hope that I may help others and give them the confidence to do the same for themselves.

I cannot tell you what my process for writing is, if there is one. My writing comes from my observations of watching the waves hit the shore, seeing a tree branch bend to a breeze, hear the far-off call of a bird, soak in the colors in the sky, a waning moon, or a rising or setting sun and how these observances manifest themselves in the feelings and emotions that pour through and out of my consciousness and spirit. Seldom is there a re-write unless to change form.

It may come from an overheard conversation, watching others interact with each other, hearing a stirring story, watching a celebration, or simply watching a squirrel jump from branch to branch. Somehow, I find comfort in this procedure. If I am troubled, it soothes me. If I am tearful, it allows me to cleanse and create all at the same time. When I am in a happy place, it makes me all the more grateful for that moment in time.

It allows me to be a small, infinitesimal part of a vast cosmos where my thoughts count, my presence in it is important at this time and space. I am reassured that this is not a fluke, but a gift from My Divine Provider—who knows all things, sees all things, and loves me anyway.

I believe He gave me this gift because I could reach so many people through my words to bring comfort, joy, empathy, sympathy, understanding, and closure when words failed them in those times of need, want, or lack. I hope I am successful—this is my intentional objective.

My words <u>are</u> my legacy…

Dedication

To my children Russell LaMont, Sr., Vaughann Christian, Heather-Michelle, and Tracey Denise, my adopted daughter and Patrick Edward, I, my son-in-law: I love you with all my heart, soul, and spirit. I am extremely proud of the adults you are becoming. I want good health, happiness, and success for you throughout the rest of your lives. Please forgive me for the mistakes I made along the way. You've turned out pretty good anyway!

To my grandchildren Russell LaMont, Jr., Patrick Edward, II, Kayla Noelle, John Elijah, India Autumn, Jalen Xavier, Kristen Alexis, Layla Ariana Saa'idah, Na-ilah Iman, Fatimah Denise, Aboubacar, Jr., and my first great-grand, Summer Rainn: I love you sooooooo much. You are the light of my life, the force that keeps my heart beating. You've been my life preservers. You have brought me untold pleasure and joy. I hope that the legacy I leave you brings you both pride for and understanding of your "Nannu". Be your best and do your best and you can conquer the world!

To my lifelong friend of 58 years, LaVonne Marie Adams-Hopkins September 29, 1929–November 25, 2014

To my English Teachers at Weequahic High School, Newark, NJ, Class of 1967, Mrs. Hannah Litzky, Mr. John Silva, et al.

To my high school mentor, Mrs. Jeanette Lappe': My undying love and respect for showing me compassion, support, and friendship throughout my young adulthood.

To my former New Jersey fans that came out to watch performances at "An Evening of Poetry and Jazz with Trishann & Friends," and who bought over 240 of my first self-published book: "Stop and Smell the Roses." Thank you so much. Your faith in me has continued to encourage me all these many years.

To all of my musician friends who tenderly and patiently guided me with their expertise to pick the best songs for each poem we performed together, especially Rio Clemente, Gordon James, Radam Schwartz, Benny Barksdale, Jr., Frederick Neal, Bradford Hayes, Cornell McGhee, Michael Logan, Rudy Walker, et al.

To the late, Rasheema Pereira, who gave me my first opportunity to share my poetry during her concerts and introduced me to her band members and allowed them to play for me. She had the voice of an angel, a true jazz deva. She is sorely missed and must be making them jam in the heavenly choir.

To my therapist Thomas J, Sandy, PsyD who put the fire under me when I would bring in pieces that I wrote to express what I was dealing with in this journey and urged me to become part of the Huntsville Literary Association to meet other artists and share my work and get a piece published in their annual chat book.

To everyone who ever agreed to listen to a poem after it was freshly written and offer opinion and criticism to make it better.

To those that want to express their love, passions and desires, but cannot find the words. It begins with the courtship, the romance, the commitment, and the consummation. It is to those that have found it and fight to keep it fresh and alive day by day.

To my parents, countless acquaintances, confidants, companions, et al (you know who you are): Thanks for abusing me sexually, emotionally, verbally, and physically, betraying my trust, breaking your promises, being dishonest, stalking me, tearing down my self-esteem, and most unforgivable of all, abandoning me. These experiences have made me stronger and more determined to survive despite your actions. You have contributed to my becoming the writer I am today. My writing became my "safe place." Without our ups and downs, and my countless hours of therapy, I wouldn't have anything to write about. I forgive you.
To Every Adult Child Survivor: I continue to dedicate this work to you who have experienced physical, emotional, verbal or sexual abuse or neglect, yet survived, by whatever means necessary, to

tell your stories so that others could gain strength and be victims no longer. I have come a long way. I am no longer a victim of my past. My hope is that others who grew up in dysfunctional families will realize that they are not alone. There are many of us who have excelled at many things despite our setbacks. Even though we were often told that we wouldn't amount to anything or that we were dumb, stupid, fat, or ugly, we had the power within to survive the heartaches and traumas to our psyches and prove all of our tormentors wrong despite occasional setbacks. As survivors, we are always on that never-ending quest to please our perpetrators, to make them proud of us. Well, the reality is that will probably never happen. We must make ourselves proud and love ourselves. If we lift our voices together, perhaps future generations of children will be spared. It is time to stop the insanity and the cycle of pain, neglect and abuse. Be Silent No Longer!

It has been a life-long dream of mine to express my innermost feelings with others in the hope that I might speak the unspoken for those who could not put pen to paper. That dream is finally being realized. It has been 54 years since I wrote my first poem. So you see, it's never too late!

Table of Contents

Introduction II
Dedication V
Table of Contents VIII

CHASING THE BEAUTY IN NATURE XIV

Stop and Smell the Roses 1
A Day at the Beach 2
Sounds 4
Spring 5
Behold! 6
Sea Breeze 7
Notice Me 8
Mist in the Mountain 9
A Season of Change 10
June 22, 2015 Monument, Colorado 12
I Wonder If 15
June 28, 2015 Monument, Colorado 16
June 29, 2015 Monument, Colorado 19
July 5, 2015 Monument, Colorado 23
July 8, 2015 Monument, Colorado 27
July 9, 2015 Monument, Colorado 28
July 10, 2015 Monument, Colorado 30
July 11, 2015 Monument, Colorado 33
You Crept into My Heart 36
Road Trip Part II 38
Even Me 40

OBSERVATIONS THAT CAUSED MY PEN TO MOVE 41

Today I Saw Your Daddy Cry 42
A New Life 44
A Mother's Morning Words of Wisdom 45
Sometimes You Get What You Ask For 46
A Prayer for My Daughter 47
A Leader with Vision 47
The Melodies of Christmas ('Tis the Season) 50
Thank You, Heavenly Father 51
The Measure of a Man Is in His Name 51
What is a Pastor? 53
There's No Place Like Home 54
The Perfect Cheer! 56
Words to PJ for High School Graduation 58

Happy 18th Birthday, PJ 60
Happy 20th Birthday, PJ 61
A Birthday Moment 62
I Could Not Wait to Tell You 63
Happy 15th Birthday, Kristen 64
The Start of Something Big 66
To My Firstborn Child, Russell 67
Road Trip Part I 68
Happy Birthday to My Daughter 70
My America 72
I Cry When 74
Guess What My Son Told Me 76
Sentiments for the New Year 76
Mothers 78
I Get to Rant, Too 80
Rant II 82
Happy New Year 2011 83
A Dream Revisited 84
Earth Revisited 85
Those Were the Good Old Days 86
My Observation of a Man of Character 87
My Grandson Is 88
My Daughter from Another Mother 89

JOURNEY IN SEARCH OF SELF 90

EXPLANATIONS, CONFRONTATIONS, AND REFLECTIONS 92

Turbulence 93
Contemplation 94
My Letter of Apologies 96
Sometimes It Sucks to be Me 104
Color Me 106
Dear Patricia, ... 108
Maybe Tomorrow 111
Open Letter to Self 112
Postscript 114
What it Means to be Lonely 115
Meditation 116
Tempest 118
Dear Mommie, June 1, 1994 120
To My Mother, Bettye M. Woolfork 123
Father's Day, June 19, 1994 124
Dear Daddy, ... 129
I Am A Survivor! 134

Dear LSJ, June, 1994 134
You Hate Me, Why? 142
Emotional Barricade 147
Requiem for a Disgruntled Housewife 148
Dear Jim, ... 154
If the Shoe Fits 156
Tick Tock 158
I Wanted to Believe 160
A Moment 161
Regret 162
Saturday Night 163
Balancing Act 164
The Journey 166
The Personal Ad 168
The Journey of a Sacred Woman 170
If My Vagina Could Talk, What Would She Say? 172
Am I Ready? 174

A PORTRAIT OF GRIEVING AND LOSS 175

My Therapist 177
The Backstory 178
When the Wailing Stopped 180
Sharing My Grief with My Facebook Friends 185
I Feel You 189
Reflection of a Friendship—The Eulogy 191
I Miss You Girl! 197
My First Xmas Without You 201
A Tribute in So Many Words 202
Eulogy for Louis Johnson Adams 203
June 26, 2015 Monument, Colorado 205
July 1, 2015 Monument, Colorado 207
I Talk to You with Pen in Hand 211
Friendship 214
The First Anniversary, November 25, 2015 215
Grief Revisited: 217
I Am a Work in Progress 217
Dear Rasheema, ... 219
Dear Stella, ... 220
Until We Meet Again 221
My Bleeding Heart 223
Loss Comes in All Forms 225
Field of Dreams 228
Dearest Susan, ... 229
For Those Left Behind 231

AN ADULT JOURNEY OF DISCOVERY **232**

LOVE AND ROMANCE **234**

    To Know You Is To 235
    I Want 236
    I Keep Holding Back 238
    First Kiss 240
    Storybook Romance 241
    My Knight in Shining Armor 242
    Transformation 243
    Love Never Fails 244
    A Wedding Day Tribute Revisited 244
    A Wedding Day Tribute: A Mother's Wish 246
    Matrimonial Journey 247
    A Four Letter Word 248
    Today is a New Day! 249
    Day Dreams of My Soldier 251
    I Should Have Told You 253
    What I Know Now 257
    Love Is 260
    I Truly Hope So 261

PASSION: HOT & SPICY **262**

    Love Dance 263
    Sunrise Interlude 264
    Work Your Magic 266
    Feels So Good 268
    Memories 270
    Retrospect 271
    What? 272
    The Two of Us 273
    The Piano Man 274
    Mr. Bass Man 274
    The Denouement 276

THE BUDDING POET **277**

    Just a Little Ditty 279
    Memories and Dreams 280
    Strong 283
    From One to Another 283
    The Sweet Memory of LaVerne 285
    A Change 287
    Search and You'll Find 287
    Triangles 289

A Ghostly Tale	*290*
I Put My Baby to Bed	291
Conclusion	293
Acknowledgments	295
About the Author	298

Savoring Eden

Chasing the Beauty in Nature

STOP AND SMELL THE ROSES

A silver balloon drifting in azure skies revels in its freedom.
Puffs of clouds float ever so slowly into the horizon.
Acres and acres of evergreens
Lift their branches in praise to a glorious sun,
And in the distance, the mountaintops caress the sky above.
Beautiful birds spread their wings and chirp merrily
In appreciation for the grandeur of it all.
Blade of grass swing back and forth in the breeze
In standing tribute to the Designer of it all.

What peace there is high atop this scenic overlook
Where man and nature tenderly embrace each the other.
Below are the hurried travelers along mazes of highway.
No time to stop and smell the roses!

How blessed we are as man
To be able to behold all of this beauty –
To touch it,
To smell it,
To see it,
To internalize with wonderment and awe,
Yet still take it all so much for granted.

Oh!
Do take the time to stop to smell the roses!
This life is, oh so, short, yet ever so sweet.
Enjoy the sunshine on your face.
Close your eyes and carefully listen
To the sounds of the universe.
Experience the kiss of the wind on your cheek.
As it runs its fingers through your hair,
Know that you've been loved –
Just look at your inheritance!

A Day at the Beach

Each day should be like a day at the beach –
Enjoying life,
Laughing, drinking cold drinks,
Eating cold chicken,
Playing tag with the waves,
Watching the ebb and flow of the tides
As they rush toward the shore.
Each day should be lived like a day at the beach –
Full of sunshine –
A warm breeze calms the senses.
The salty air invigorates and has restorative power.

Each day should be lived like a day at the beach –
Where people share the pleasantries of a smile,
A warm greeting.
The beautiful colors of the umbrellas
Blowing in the breeze
Pale in comparison to the rainbow of colors
On the sunbathers and water players.

Each day should be lived like a day at the beach –
Enjoying the place where the water seems to touch the sky.
The darkness of the water lovingly caresses
The paleness of the crystal blue expanse.

Smiling faces,
Sand-covered bodies,
Windswept, sand sprinkled hair,
Bathing suits full of sand
Are all a part of the beauty of the day.
Even the broken shells on the shore
Enhance the beauty of a day at the beach.
Each day should be lived like a day at the beach –
It is special – not often to be enjoyed.
Well worth the trip, the traffic, and the parking fees.
Today we commune with nature.

Savoring Eden

We touch our soul selves.
We throw off our prejudices.
We don't worry about our bodies, or
The troubles we left at home.
How nice it would be . . .
If each day could be lived like a day at the beach!

SOUNDS

I listen to the peaceful, calming music,
and suddenly,
I am in another dimension.
I close my eyes and listen to
the resonance of the violins and
I see birds soaring
through bright blue skies above me.
I hear the whisper of the wind in the trees.
I can even hear
the merriment of little children at play.

The flutes are making sweet melody.
I see and hear lovers
Running across clover covered meadows
Smiling
Laughing
Embracing.

I open my eyes,
but briefly,
and close them again to listen.
The music of the universe soothes me.

My thoughts turn to beautiful things:
Butterflies,
Flowers
Cheerful greens,
Tranquil blues,
Sunsets,
Starlight,
Love.

The sounds of nature fill my head.

SPRING

Today is a good day.
The skies are clear.
The air is fresh.
The birds soar through snow-white clouds.
The flowers are peaking through the earth.

Children play in the great outdoors.
People walk the streets with smiling faces.
The troubles of yesterday are momentarily forgotten
Because the grass is growing again,
And the trees are adorned with buds.

Spring has come and with its arrival –
Awareness,
Beauty,
Hope,
Rebirth.
Tread lightly in its footprints.

It truly is a good day!

BEHOLD!

Cool sand under my feet . . .
White water spray upon my face . . .
Serenity enfolds me,
As I listen to the waves caress the shore.

I walk the beach
And stare out to the place
Where sea and sky become one.
I imagine . . .
A time long past
When life first touched the shore.

Acres and acres of crystalline sand –
Miles of clear blue skies and
Blue-green waters.
Can you imagine . . .

The beauty the first pair of eyes beheld?

SEA BREEZE

White water spray
>   plants gentle kisses upon my face.

The cool sea breeze
>   embraces me tenderly.

Sea and sky unite
>   as the harbor lights play love melodies.

The waves
>   seem to ebb and flow to my heartbeat.

The moon smiles,
>   very pleased with itself,
>   as it beholds the lovers' embrace.

The stars shine brightly
>   having granted ever so many wishes.
>   "Star-Light, Star-Bright. . . ."

White water spray
>   washes some of my cares away, but

The cool sea breeze
>   *reminds* me . . .

>   You are not here with me tonight.

NOTICE ME

The clouds drift through azure skies.
The sun plants its kiss gently upon my face.
The wind sends its caressing breeze through my hair,
And the grass beneath my feet lovingly strokes my toes.

What a wonderful day!
Nature and man peacefully communing with each other,
Because Nature has called, "time out".
She says, "Enjoy my pleasures, today.
Pay attention to my beauty –
Quickly . . .
Before it fades away.
Store this day in your memory bank
And draw upon it in times of stress,
Or when I am not at my best.
Remember our good days together, and
Forgive the bad."
What a wonderful day?
Only one of many yet to come.

MIST IN THE MOUNTAIN

Terrified travel
Through winding roads
Of heavily laden fog.
Wooden fingers of naked branches
Reach out in the gloom
To consume my soul.
My heart is racing
Trying to find the lines on the pavement
Through blurred windshield and tattered wipers.

Upon arrival
A sigh of relief escapes in my exhalation.
Safety restored
Until the lonely ride back home.

The beauty does not escape me
Here atop Burritt on the Mountain.
I peer through floor to ceiling windows
Into the fog that is so thick
It now looks like snow falling
Upon the exposed tendrils of branches.
I am watching the visitors meander
Down pathways
Able to enjoy themselves.
Despite the falling mist and
Invisibility of the landscape.

Mesmerizing, yet mystifying all at once.
A moment in time –
A frightening, yet inspiring vision of . . .
The many complexions of the "She"
We call "Mother Nature."

Patricia Ann Woolfork

A SEASON OF CHANGE

Time has been pushed forward –
A prelude to the coming of Spring,
Nature reinvents itself after a long winter's nap.
Baby animals will arrive soon, and
The crocus and daffodils will defy the last vestiges of
Winter's begrudging retreat.
People will reemerge from their woolen coats and boots
With a sigh of relief – from a season of
Shoveling, shivering, and salting icy walks and driveways.
Soon the sun will shine brighter.
The sky will seem bluer.
Their desire for warmth will be fulfilled.

With Nature's rebirth comes the renewal of spirit –
The ritual of changing out closets and dresser drawers,
Cleaning the walls, windows and woodwork,
Getting the tools ready for planting and pruning, and
Gassing up the mower instead of the snow blower –
The smells of pine and chlorine permeate the air.

Ahhhhhhh –
The forecast is for rising temperatures and a chance of rain.
No more slush and ice – unless you mean the eating kind!
Even the birds have returned and
Bless the air with musical entertainment.
And, as for us mere mortals –
Vows are renewed to fulfill our New Year's Resolutions,
Shed our winter fat for that special occasion, or
The swimsuit, that's coming;
Purge the fog from our Winter brains, and
Ascend from our dens of Winter Madness,
Cabin Fever and Seasonal Depression.
At last, Spring is on the horizon –
We have survived the Arctic blast!
We are steeled in our resolve to fix that fence,
Clean the gutters, replace that broken hose,

Savoring Eden

Change out the batteries, throw open the windows, and
Let the freshened air inside.

The time for Reflection has also arrived.
What will or can we do better in this new season of our lives?
Will we prune our old way of thinking and
Replace it with forgiveness and reconciliation?
Will we weed out negativity, and
Turn over the soil of our past and
Fertilize it with love of self and others,
Happiness,
Prosperity, and
Good health?

In this Season of Change –
Will we finish our "to do" list?
Author a "bucket" list, or plan our legacy?
Will we turn to Divine guidance?
Will we believe in our potential and self-worth?
Time has been moved forward –
Are we motivated to do the same?

Patricia Ann Woolfork

June 22, 2015
Monument, Colorado

I watch the large black crow fly among
the tall slender pines and shimmering aspen trees
from the front porch of this Rocky Mountain home
as I listen to the wind chimes
and gaze upon the puffs of white
mixed into the azure skies above me.

I am at peace among these trees
feeling the cool breeze
of the mountain air upon my sandaled feet.
I watch the fronds
from the still unopened blooms
sway from side to side
among the yard statues of angels and imps.
I hear the birds chirping, the crow cawing,
the whine of a garage door closing
on the gray stuccoed, almost mansion-sized,
house across the cul-de-sac.

I don't remember ever hearing
the sound that the crow makes,
ebony feathers glistening
through the blades of uncut grass.
There seem to be lots of crows in the area –
a veritable symphony
of communication among them.
Occasionally, I hear the barking of a neighbor's dog
which breaks into the intermittent silence
reminding me that they, too
are enjoying this beauty in nature.

The pine cones display a golden hue – not brown
like I am accustomed to seeing back home –
their tips pointing upward toward the sky
scattered upon the majestic branches of 50+ feet

of brown/gray trunks and radiant green needles
also reaching upward as if giving reverence to its Creator.

There is another bird making a staccato type chirp,
another in the distance answering in kind.
The ting of the chime, almost temple like,
adds the punctuation mark to the end of the discourse.
One, two, three, four
in perfect time,
each continuing sound
growing more faint
until the next breeze
reanimates it and the ritual is repeated.

I hear the occasional sound of a car
travelling up or down the winding road –
the only reminder
of civilization outside the wooden oasis.
Far away voices travel up the hill,
perhaps of neighbors
further down the cul-de-sac –
probably unaffected by the beauty around them
because this is their everyday habitat,
and they are
not as impressed as I
to be able to observe it with fresh eyes
and enjoy its grace and beauty.

The deep woof of a faraway dog
interrupts my thoughts.
What is disturbing its peace . . .
a deer, a bear, or some other woodland creature?

Ants and flies go about their business,
as do I, as I make my observations,
write upon these pages and
reflect on how truly blessed I am today . . .
to have awakened in my right mind,
not as stiff as yesterday,

Patricia Ann Woolfork

able to see more clearly
because my numbers are better,
more hopeful,
more thankful,
more positive,
feeling loved beyond measure
and happy
– no, content –
– yes, happy –
to be me and for my blessings.

I Wonder If

I wonder if
Nature ever tires of being underappreciated?
Does the sun tire of shining upon people
That takes its brilliance for granted?
Does the moon get sick and tired of hanging out all day
Just to get its chance to show off in the evening sky?
Does it resent having to share the spotlight
With the stars and other celestial bodies?
Is Nature crying when it rains?
Is she utterly enraged when it storms and the wind blows
And the earth moves
Because she has been ignored, devalued, and abused?

Or, is she just another tired mother. . .
Weary of working day in and out
Year after year to provide for her children?
It is true that they did not ask to be here, but
Would it kill them to say a kind word,
Make a gesture of appreciation and unconditional love,
Make her feel special and needed –
Not just an afterthought –
Just something else that has to be tolerated –
A burden – An inconvenience?

Wouldn't it be better to commend her for her
Faithfulness,
Endurance,
Fortitude, and Beauty
Without complaint?
Consider this:
For everything there is a reason as well as a season, but
Without Her there would be no You.

June 28, 2015
Monument, Colorado

Voices echo up and down the cul-de-sac.
A woman in a big, yellow hat
takes her morning constitutional down
the winding paved road.
The crows are at their cawing again
sending code to one another.
The faint chirp of another bird is drowned out
by the cacophony made by the crows.
Their noise is punctuated by the bark of a far-off dog,
its peace constantly interrupted by
this constant conversation.

The houses almost disappear among the landscape.
They are colored like nature –
grays, browns, taupe, and
autumnal hues of orange and gold –
Brick, stucco, and wooden planks fit so effortlessly
behind the shade of the evergreen pines,
the aspens and occasional willow.
Driveways are lined with stones and rocks, and the
yards accented with stoned walls and embankments.

WOOF, CAW, chirp, buzz, WOOF, small dog – yap!
The only other sound I hear in this magical place
is the scurrying the squirrel makes
going through the grass on its mission to reach a tree.

An occasional butterfly crosses my line of vision
– the jewel of radiant color –
that compliments the hanging baskets of begonias and
garden flora of pinks, reds, yellows, and oranges
that are visible across the road.

Tranquility is the word I'd use for this bath of beauty
I find myself luxuriating in this fine morning.

Savoring Eden

How can anyone truly believe
that this all happened by accident?
It is as though a very skilled artist
tipped his brush into his palette
and made broad strokes to create
the blue mixed with white to form the sky;
dabbed into the earth tones
to punctuate the horizon
with the peaks and valleys of the mountain range,
then decided to cap the tallest one
with just a touch of white
to make it just that much more majestic.
Then he colored the ground
with greens, reds, and browns
so that our eyes could be amazed
by the proliferation of color
making them able to jump from one color to the next
with the motion of a wave,
the ripple on the surface of the water
– rocking us gently –
in the arms of natural wonder.

Our senses cannot help but be awakened
in this mountainous paradise.
Sight, sound, smells, even taste,
are equally entertained.

The wind is still today.
The chimes on the porch barely move.
The flies have taken their turn today,
buzzing around me as I write.
I do hear the crickets though
as I watch a solitary ant weave back and forth
across the concrete porch
searching for a path back into the garden.

One might think the fly to be a pest, and
it really is, but it serves a purpose also.
It interrupts my consciousness and

Patricia Ann Woolfork

alerts me to the other sounds surrounding me
I may have overlooked without
the persistent annoyance of this singular pesky fly!

The sun is warm on my feet although
the rest of me is hidden in the shade.
I feel really alive!
My words cannot fully express
my wonderment and awe.
Yet, I try to convey
what my sight and senses tell me as
the wisp of a breeze caresses my ear,
tenderly kisses my neck,
and makes the chime sing again as if . . .
My Creator
UNDERSTANDS . . .
EVERYTHING . . .
I've written on this page!

JUNE 29, 2015
MONUMENT, COLORADO

I returned to Colorado Springs
twenty-one years ago on a vacation
for a cross-country ski trip for the blind
in Aspen and Vale with a very dear friend.
I had been gone for over eighteen years.
I returned to New Jersey in 1976 after my divorce.

Today I found my old home – still standing –
the yard overgrown and the fencing moved –
It was no longer considered the best part of town,
but the park at the end of the street
was now Memorial Park, with monuments and plaques,
complete with a recreation center and a motor track –
a tribute to all service personnel from the area
who had given their lives from WWII to the present –
Fireworks light up the sky from this location and
people come from near and far to observe the fanfare.
There were still boats on the lake.
People were skiing and fishing.
It was both reverential and stunningly beautiful.

It was an awesome re-experience to look from my yard
Turn right and see the top of Pike's Peak
in its entire majestic splendor
 – faint traces of snow still visible in the heat of June –
Turn left and see
the glistening lake and monuments with flags waving.

On a lark,
I wanted to see if my neighbor was still living there,
and, to my surprise, she was.
It was such a lovely reunion.
We talked about –
how she taught me how to garden,
how to dress a rabbit,

how to put up pickles, and about
how to take "the pill"
– a thing we both got wrong –
because my daughter was conceived.

We laughed, we hugged,
exchanged numbers, and
made promises to keep in touch.
I was so moved by this experience.
How blessed I was to see her again –
frail from aging and hard work,
but still alert, comical, and friendly at 82 years old.

The Garden of the Gods was next on the re-visit.
I was driven around the massive red rocks
The Kissing Camels, The Balanced Rock,
shooting up from the earth like prehistoric dinosaurs.
Wild and tame at the same time!
There are trails for bikers, hikers and cycles of all kinds.
Everywhere – blue skies with bright white clouds –
– beige and green mixed in with the rock formations –
Pike's Peak in the distance –
– sunshine and cool breezes tossing my hair –
Man and nature communing with respect and admiration.

I rode through Manitou Springs where 21 years ago
I tasted the mineral water and purchased
my deerskin boots and Stetson hat.
We weaved through the streets of Old Colorado Springs,
The Downtown District where I worked
for the power company,
The Historic District where I lived
in my first apartment as a new bride in 1969, and
then drove pass the hospital
where two of my children were born.
Lunch was at a barbeque joint called "Rudy's."
and, like any good westerner,
we consumed brisket and ribs Yum!
Fond and sad memories

Savoring Eden

passed through space and time
as I retraced my steps made over 46 years ago.
Remembering . . .
How we brought our first child
from the base hospital at Fort Carson
to our new home
which we purchased at only 21 years old.

Remembering . . .
Mowing our double- lot property,
picking fruit from the trees on it, and
feeding the squirrel
that used to scratch on the back screen each day
to take a peanut from my hand.

Remembering . . .
Drinking root beer out of champagne glasses,
too poor to afford the real thing,
listening to Motown
on the rug in front of the fireplace March 7, 1973,
the day our daughter was conceived
(ergo the "pill" misinformation).

Satiated and happy,
we made our way back to Monument
to rehash the day,
enjoy the warm breeze on the back deck,
play fetch with Tillie,
experience the aroma of the tall pines,
the musicality of the singing birds,
see yet another crow, and hear the patches
of conversation from the surrounding neighbors.
It's funny –
in the woods, voices seem to project
in the openness of the outdoors.
No one seems to whisper –
yet no one intentionally listens to the other.
We seem to be in our own little oasis of
space,

time, and
being.

Remembering . . .
the good,
the bad, and
the ugly –
A time capsule reopened in 2015.

July 5, 2015
Monument, Colorado

I am sitting on the deck with my breakfast and coffee
looking at the slender pines that adorn the yard.
I am relaxing with my two new best friends,
Ollie, (Oliver) a Shih Tzu and
Tillie, (Mathilda), a Golden Lab/Shepherd mix.
We are listening to a lawnmower in the distance
and the faint chirps of the birds.
Tillie is off and running.
She sees something in the grass
that stimulates her curiosity.
Ollie, older,
just grazes in some grass almost as tall as he.

I see a neighbor across the expanse of yard.
A young boy, maybe fourteen,
is the one using the mower,
doing his assigned chores perhaps.
The sound of the mower
is the only disturbance to the tranquility of these woods.
The breeze is gentle this morning.
I can only see the tops of the trees sway just a little.
Ollie and Tillie patiently await
the drop of a morsel from my plate –
not happening guys!

I see the silk of a web
glisten in the sun from one of the deck posts.
Another neighbor's yard art is spinning.
Its copper discs are illuminated by
the sun shining upon them.
Their movement is hypnotic and
peaceful at the same time.
I see the rustle of a squirrel's tail
in the distance as it climbs the massive tree trunk.
A beige sedan comes flying down the curved road.

Patricia Ann Woolfork

It is Sunday morning.
They must be late for church.
Its presence disturbs the dogs.
It's coming back up the hill.
They must have forgotten something.

The neighbors directly across the yard
have adorned their tiny patio
with hanging baskets of flowers and a hummingbird feeder.
Two squirrels are chasing each other in their yard.
A yellow butterfly gently touches down
on a cluster of pine needles.
There are three squirrels in a tree
jumping from limb to limb
going even higher, dangling, leaping, chattering.
Tillie finds something to bark about
on the other side of the yard
and Ollie follows.
Oh, a rabbit is hopping in the grass on my right.
I hope Tillie doesn't see it.

The neighbor across the street
in the gray stucco house has returned
and removes packages from her car.
I barely can see the movement from this vantage point,
but every sound catches my attention.

The squirrel family is very vocal, their tails flapping.
The noisy one must be the mother
and the kids are not listening.
They are too busy wanting to play.
One can only speculate.
I don't speak squirrel!

I see another bunny in the neighbor's yard.
Its little white tail is highlighted by the sun.
I watch trying to see if it reappears
toward the front of the house.
No such luck.

Savoring Eden

Oh, there it is again getting closer to the road.
It's hard to see it in
the camouflage of browns, tans, and greens.

An even larger rabbit hops across our yard now.
I try not to make a sound because
I don't want Tillie to see it.
However, I do believe it is outside of
the perimeter of the invisible fence.
It made it!
Tillie is lying at my feet.

Two more bunnies
hop across the side yard again
going behind the neighbor's house.
A single bunny comes back
and hops toward the road and disappears in the shrubs.
Another one, even smaller, makes the same trek,
barely visible with its light brown fur.
Their home must be somewhere in that cluster of shrubbery.
They are so cute!

The bunnies are back and Tillie is off!
She hears them, but they are beyond her reach.
She doesn't bark.
She just stands, as if on point,
awaiting the next movement in the shrubs,
sniffing the air.
A bunny has completely crossed the road.
Hippity-hoppity,
it goes into the open field,
as if tauntingly saying,
"You can't catch me."

Yet another car comes down the road, barely audible.
It sounds more like a strong wind.
It must be a newer model.
The breeze is so soft on my skin.
I could go to sleep now that my belly is full,

and the movement in the aspen trees is so beautiful.
Their leaves seem to shimmer –
like the dance of a ballerina –
graceful.

A big crow flies into our yard and
perches in the pine tree in front of me.
Buzzing, chirping,
chattering, squeaking –
crickets have awakened.
Running, hopping,
flittering, scurrying,
barking, whining, tweeting –
these are the sounds
outside this Rocky Mountain home.

Tillie spots a blue bird and chases it,
but it regains its altitude and gets away.
So again she comes to lay near my feet
in the cool breeze on this wooden deck
in this marvelous wonder of nature
called, Monument, Colorado.

JULY 8, 2015
MONUMENT, COLORADO

Even the fog
Makes a glorious appearance
High up in these Rocky Mountains.
Like a bridal veil,
Its mist obscures the craggy beauty of the ridges
And adorns them in a glistening haze.

One wonders from this distance if
It is raining up on the Peak,
Or
      If snow
            Is falling
                  Once again.

It has been unseasonably cold the past few days,
So it is a possibility.

I won't know
Which it is
Until I go outdoors, again,
Tomorrow
To see
What wonders
Await me.

July 9, 2015
Monument, Colorado

A.M.
I have just one more full day in Colorado. I will use it to explore some areas I may have overlooked. Our plan is to visit some quaint shops in Downtown Monument. They have antique and thrift shops there. Wish I had brought a larger suitcase.

I've had my breakfast, and I am dressed and ready to go. Tillie and Ollie were groomed yesterday, and we have already had our play time. They will go to the doggy daycare today. Hopefully, they will still smell fresh this afternoon.

I am reminded of my blessings as I write upon this page: Yesterday I had a full-body massage. Oh, if only I could do that every week! I had my dinner at a 50's inspired diner called "Rosie's" complete with jukeboxes on each table. I slept fairly well. I went to bed early for a change and I awaken refreshed. My knee still wants to act the fool, though!

We have been invited to dinner with another family this evening. I have become quite the social butterfly, huh? I hope I can make this happen when I get back to Alabama. I have been given some ideas on how to make it happen from my new acquaintances. Wish me luck.

P.M.
What a beautiful day! We took Tillie and Ollie to Camp Bow Wow for a play day. Then we went to Downtown Monument—approximately six blocks long! We went to a high-priced boutique and home décor store, and, believe it or not, I found a dollhouse miniature store. I salivated over the tiny treasures and bemoaned my not having my three dollhouses with me in Huntsville yet. I settled on some back issues of "Dollhouse Miniature," and the latest copy as one of my souvenirs of my Colorado visit. We then went to lunch at a lovely winery/restaurant where we sampled four different wines. I had a yellow and red beet salad with goat cheese

and candied nuts and cheddar/bacon soup. Jacque had the smoked salmon, onion and capers brochette, and the Swiss onion soup. Everything was delicious, and the waiter was a blond cutie (male, of course).

After lunch, we went to Santa Fe Jewelry and The Hangar Thrift Shop, and another small shop where I found a pair of framed needlepoint roses and a lovey music box.

We picked up the dogs, watched Wheel of Fortune and Jeopardy before we were picked up to go to yet another dinner at a friend and neighbor's house just one house above the gray stucco house I talked about earlier.

Our hosts were Arlene and Norm Kraemer. Their home was awesome. It had a Spanish tiled roof, and the inside was perfectly South Western with adobe styled walls and arches, a South Western fireplace, beautiful artwork, and a copper water fountain in the foyer.

Our hors d'oeuvres were a warm spinach onion cheese dip with pita chips, a veggie platter with onion dip and potato chips, and, of course, wine. The main course was a meat and spinach lasagna, fresh steamed green beans, Italian bread, and a salad of cubed watermelon and mango over a bed of baby spinach and arugula. More wine, of course. Dessert was a pound cake topped fresh blueberries and real whipped cream, and coffee with Bailey's Irish Cream.

I had another scare with my glucose before dinner. It was 55mg. I drank some orange juice and then ate like a piglet (ha ha). I am a contented tourist!

We had such great conversation and laughed a lot. Turns out that both Arlene and Norm are only children, too! We exchanged numbers and promised to keep in touch, and they would keep an eye on Jacque for me. Norm even offered to take me to Denver for my flight on Saturday if my arranged ride falls through.

I will pack early in the a.m. wash a final load of clothes and get ready to enjoy my last day in Colorado. I have taken my insulin and put on my PJs and finished my entry into this missal.

I must remind Jacque to go to the bank and take out the trash.

Good night, book.

July 10, 2015
Monument, Colorado*

Tears well up in my eyes
and blur my vision as I watch
the swaying of the aspen tree in the neighbor's yard
across from the deck, and then
I look upward across the road to the red tiled,
Spanish style home where I had dinner
with the neighbors last night, and
I realize that this is the last day
that I will sit here on this beautiful deck and
watch the pine trees dance in the crisp mountain air,
listen to the birds chirp,
play with Tillie throwing the long rope,
playing catch and fetch
with Ollie on my lap peacefully resting.

A tender breeze moves through the wet grass,
so beautifully green, because
it has rained for the last three days.
I watch the yard art spinning in the distance.
The neighbor has added another piece,
and its movement is also mesmerizing.
Tillie is huffing now, tired from our play,
and Ollie, is just Ollie, lying on my lap.

I am going to miss this place.
It has brought me peace of mind and showed me
God's beauty and the majesty of His creation.
I watch the clouds slowly drift across the sky,
the sky more white than blue, but the various shades of blue
are sprinkled throughout the expanse like fairy dust.

I watch the neighbor replenish the hummingbird feeder.
She waters her baskets of flowers
before returning inside her mountain retreat.
The German Shepherd in the adjacent yard

suddenly appears
through its doggy door to enjoy the day.

I hear the sound of faraway traffic.
A car is coming up the road.
I can see it – a streak of white
cutting through the trees
followed by another – a red one this time.
My awareness becomes more acute and
amazes me when I sit quietly and listen.

Thank you, Father for this privilege.
Thank you, Father for my vision.
Thank you, Father for the gift you have given me.
Thank you, Father for this friendship
that you have put into place.
We will talk later when
I get my book and
write these words upon its pages.

These words were dictated into my smartphone and later transcribed as best as I could decipher through my tears and sobs.

July 11, 2015
Monument, Colorado

Sleep did not come easily for me last night.
The anticipation of going home grew heavy
while trying to shove all of my belongings into one little bag,
a daunting task at best.
The thought of leaving my friend and
this mountain greenery
was distressing to me on several levels.

I was at peace here,
and my friend still needs support after losing her husband.
I watched her sink further into depression
as the days of my departure grew closer,
and I knew it would not be easy
for either of us to say good-bye.

The alarm went off at 4:00 a.m.
I showered and dressed and
put the remainder of my belongings into two suitcases
and a tote bag.
Jacque made me a frozen omelet,
a slice of toast, and a cup of coffee.

When her step-granddaughter arrived
to transport me to the airport, it was 5:30 a.m.
We hugged.
We fought back tears.
It was difficult for us to let go of each other.
I told her that my next trip out
would be for pleasure instead of grief,
she should remember to eat and take her medicine, and
get out of the house often.
Good-byes can be so tedious and traumatic.

Patricia Ann Woolfork

The ride to Denver International was uneventful
although we did miss one turn.
I took pictures on the way.
We laughed.
I told her to look after her grandmother for me.
I thanked her for picking me up
and driving me nearly an hour
on her birthday – just another example of the
complete acceptance and love I received
from this entire network of family and friends
of my new sister/friend.

Denver International is huge!
It took nearly twenty minutes –
two elevators, two train rides,
and one transporter cart to get to Gate B24.
I am on United Flight 504 to Nashville.
I should play these numbers
when I get to Nashville
before the two-hour drive back to Huntsville.
We don't have the lottery in Alabama.
Wouldn't it be great if I won?

It is 9:30 a.m. and we are boarding.
I have a window seat.
Maybe I should take a nap, or
maybe I'll just look out of the window.
With one,
I can dream about the beauty I have enjoyed.
With the other,
I can wipe the tears from my cheeks
as they descend
        down my face
                as the plane ascends into the sky.

I am left with beautiful memories and
a panoramic view of where
I have been for the last three weeks.
I saw my first sunrise this morning,

awesome in its brilliance of yellow, red, and orange.
It reminded me, once again,
of the beauty of a southwestern sky.
No wonder so many pictures
have been painted about it.
How could an artist not be inspired
by the variance of hues, the textures of the rocks,
red and brown, covered in greenery,
pines saluting the heavens, and
aspens dancing in the breeze?

The sun shines upon my naked wrist as
I write these words.
I listen to the overhead compartments click shut,
They have started the engines now.
The plane has been fully packed, "a full flight, "
we are told over the loud speaker.
I take pictures of a food truck as it detaches itself.
It slowly backs away from the plane.
I eagerly await the take off.
That's the best part!
We start our slow-paced back up away from the ramp
to make the turn toward the runway.
I feel a nap coming on, but I am too excited.

I want to take pictures of the voluminous clouds, and
the landscape as it gets smaller and smaller
as we go higher and higher.

I love the thrill I get when we
Taxi down the runway,
Pick up speed,
Lift off, and
         Soar up into the sky
                           Like a great, silver bird!

Patricia Ann Woolfork

YOU CREPT INTO MY HEART

You crept into my heart on pink-padded feet
4 ounces, rain soaked, flea infested,
Eyes encrusted with infection –
A little mound of tiger stripes and spots, and
Patches of brown, white, and orange.

I carefully bathed you until
The water ran clear of dirt and fleas.
I knew why your birth mom had easily abandoned you
Without consideration of your potential.
She carted off your siblings from the overturned
Plastic trashcan in my backyard and left you to die.

I lovingly wrapped you in a towel and dried your fur.
I kept you swaddled in a clean, dry baby's blanket,
And held you close to my chest
So you could hear my heartbeat as you slept.
Here in the palm of my hand
Was a newly born creature of God
Beautifully clothed and adorned
In little white boots and a pink nose.
It was love in an instant!

The next day I took you to the vet.
In his assistant's haste to clean your eyes,
An eyeball was ruptured – I gasped, fearful.
Surely now you must have to be put down!
Tears streaming down my face,
I waited for the doctor to confirm my suspicions –
Only to discover that you could
Lead a "purrfectly" normal life with one eye.
With that vision locked into my mind's eye,
I foresaw a cat with a patch over its eye,
Pirate-like, I suppose.
So I named you "Patches."
To say that you can see

Savoring Eden

As good as any feline with two eyes
Would be an understatement!
You get into as much mischief as any cat can!
And, most importantly,
You can see how much I love you!

It's been nearly five years since we became family.
And on those occasional stormy, rainy nights
You climb into my bed and find your way onto my chest
To listen to my heartbeat, or
You curl your body into the curve of my side and
Rest your head on my arm and sleep peacefully.

At those times I wonder
If you remember the day you were
Rescued from the storm
Rescued from abandonment and certain death –
I wonder if you know . . .
We both were.
I needed unconditional love.
I needed someone or something
To greet me with genuine affection,
To show me I have really been missed,
To cheer me up with antics, and
To comfort me through sickness or sadness
With closeness and companionship.
Yes,
You crept into my life
On little pink-padded feet and
Captured my heart forever.

Patches is now eighteen years old, and still acts like a kitten. To my amazement, when I moved to Alabama six years ago and took her to a vet, I was told she could see perfectly fine out of both eyes.

Road Trip Part II

Deep within the grasp of darkness
One must find ways to combat the feeling of
Impending insanity
Caused by the monotony of the insipid drone of the
Soundtrack playing ping pong inside your skull . . .
"How much longer?"
"Is that all the far I have gotten?"
Et cetera, et cetera, et cetera.
You watch the clock on the dashboard
And try to remember what time zone you are in.

I choose to focus on the change of colors in the sky
As morning light dances with the waning moonlight
And fog descends from the mountaintops
To form the dew that plants kisses on the ground below –
The first signs of a new day approaching.

Streaks of orange appear in the horizon
As the sun slowly begins to manifest itself
And stirs my resolve to have a better day, today,
Than yesterday.

The sky is turning from black to navy to azure
As the sun grins through the reappearing clouds
Which have been shrouded in the darkness.

Birds in flight, have arisen from their slumber
To find sustenance for their young
Before the summer's heat overtakes us all.

I remember . . .
I am covered by Grace,
Bestowed with Mercy,
Protected by Sacrifice,
To be a true reflection of His Goodness.

Savoring Eden

His presence is in the fully risen sun
Shining brightly above a mountain in the distance,
Casting its reflection on scattered tributaries,
And now streaming through the car's visors
As if to say,
"Good Morning."

Car after car join me in parade down the highway
Toward jobs in factories and offices,
Car lots and convenience stores –
Giving me more reason
To be more mindful of our safety
And the destination
On this road trip called life.

EVEN ME

Every opening blossom,
Every dancing bee,
Every leaf and blade of grass
Is beautiful
In the eyes of the Creator.
Even me,
I am beautiful!

The cracks in the earth,
The slug on the pavement,
The weeds in the garden,
The ants at a picnic,
The black widow spider,
The skunk and the snake
All have a purpose –
Are part of a Divine Plan.
Even me,
I have a reason for being.

The thunder that frightens,
The winds that blow,
The torrential rains
Every time I laugh or cry,
Sing or sigh, or
Write a poem
Is an event of
Monumental importance
To someone,
Even me!

Observations that Caused my Pen to Move

Patricia Ann Woolfork

TODAY I SAW YOUR DADDY CRY

I saw a miracle today, and . . .
I saw your daddy cry!
They were not the normal tears
We hear about these days –
Tears over wasted youth,
Gang violence, early incarceration, and
Untimely death!

I saw a proud father and a promising son,
Who, through his father's guidance,
Had propelled himself forward
toward a life of success with a full scholarship
to a prestigious school!

Maybe he is the first in the family to go to college,
Or maybe the money was funny.
Who knows the full story?
But today, the story of pride and gratitude
Was written on both of their faces
As they stood before the congregation
In joyous, thankful praise before
The One Who Makes All Things Possible!

Yes, I saw your daddy cry today.
As an empathizing tear
Made slow tracks down my face, I thought
A more beautiful sight could not have been beheld
Unless you count the time
This father first laid his eyes upon this precious son.

I witnessed you take that symbolic step,
Away from your dad,
As our pastor had instructed.
This is the first step you take toward manhood.

Savoring Eden

Though he will never be far behind,
The support and love you have received, thus far,
Will sustain you in the years ahead.

Someday you will shed tears with your son or daughter.
They will be tears of joy, pride, and appreciation, too.
Remember this day.
This is the day I saw your daddy cry!

*Dedicated to Mr. Darren Ware and son,
Sunday, February 6, 2011, and presented at
Mount Vernon Missionary Baptist Church,
Newark, NJ*

A New Life

Once on a quiet, restful summer's evening
The heavens seemed full of bright shining luminaries.
The night was calm.
There was a touch of awe in the air.
There was peace.
The most beautiful event of life had just taken place.

A new being,
A new soul,
A new creation had just arrived.
One of God's greatest miracles had manifested itself,
And it had happened to me

On that quiet, restful summer evening
It was not the birth of an infant,
But rather the birth of an adult.
I had finally found my purpose.
I would deal with reality rather than fantasy.
I would be wise instead of foolish.
I would find strength not weakness –
Hope and Faith when there seems to be none.

Yes, on that quiet summer evening
That new being,
That new soul,
That new life,
Became mine.

A Mother's Morning Words of Wisdom

I know you are not a morning person, but
I am awake and thinking about you.
I want you to know that I love you and that
I hope you have a wonderfully beautiful day today.
I hope that God's Grace and Mercy
Are showered down upon you,
And that you share that Goodness with others.

I tell you this from a mother's prospective –
Just trying to impart some wisdom.
In the large scheme of things,
You really don't have it so bad.
You have a great job you love to do.
You have three beautiful, talented, and intelligent children,
Your husband loves you, and he also has a great job.
Remember your volunteer experience –
The day at the soup kitchen?

I am reminded how fragile life can be,
And that we are only here for a short time.
That is why it is critical
That we use that time wisely and lovingly
With those and to those we care about the most –
Especially me!
Just think of the person who no longer has a mother.
Do you ever envision your world without me in it?
Now may be the time to start thinking about that.

Praise God, Be Thankful, and Full of Gratitude
For all that you do have –
Remember . . .
Tomorrow is just another one of God's gifts.
Only He can decide who gets it.   XOXOXO, Mom

Patricia Ann Woolfork

SOMETIMES YOU GET WHAT YOU ASK FOR

Forty-two years ago after the birth of two sons,
I found myself pregnant with an eight-month-old on my hip.
Back then there were no sonograms.
You took what you got.
Couldn't pick out the layette – so
You picked green and yellow.
I kept telling my friends, "I want a little girl, and
If it is, I want you to bring me a frilly pink dress and
A pair of gold hoops to the hospital
For me to bring her home."

After a fast and brutal labor,
I welcomed Heather-Michelle into the world
Followed by near-death post-delivery complications.
When I awakened a day later,
I had gotten my wish, and
I had the dress and the earrings, too.

So today, I am basking in that memory –
Remembering the joy of being able to go to term
Despite all the risks against being able to do so, and
I have a beautiful little girl for my trouble.
Happy Birthday!

A PRAYER FOR MY DAUGHTER

Dear Woman of God:
Be still for a while and praise God for His favor,
His grace and His awesomeness.
God is able to do the impossible and always near.
He loves us unconditionally.

Together, let's praise Him with one voice.
Let's say this prayer: Dear God,
This is my daughter, whom I love, and
This is my prayer for her.
Help her live her life to the fullest.
Please promote her and
Cause her to excel above her expectations.
Help her to shine in the darkest places
Where it is hard to love.
Protect her at all times.
Lift her up when she needs You the most.
Let her know
When she walks with You,
She will always be safe.
Amen.

    Jeremiah 29:11:
"For I know the plans I have for YOU, declares the Lord."

Patricia Ann Woolfork

A LEADER WITH VISION

A leader with vision finds the way
To inspire and empower others for success.
A leader with vision finds a place
For every gender, ethnicity, and social status.

A leader with a vision works for and with others
For the common good and betterment of all.

A leader with a vision seeks out others
With an entrepreneurial spirit,
Promotes self-esteem,
Motivates, and stimulates the exchange of ideas.

A leader with a vision finds ways
To improve efficiency.

A leader with vision is
One who saw the way to the top
And took no detours no matter how rough the journey.

A leader with vision
Knows how to empathize and sympathize,
Knows how to delegate,
Knows how to
Recognize and bring out the talent in others
Because of their own life's experiences.

A leader with vision sees
The possibility, not the negativity,
And aggressively pursues
The best in self and others.

A leader has been there – done that!
A leader has been on the front line.
A leader has counted the costs and doesn't look back.
Do you see what I see?

Savoring Eden

Do you hear what I hear?
I see a leader in the making.
I hear change coming.

Will you follow the leader?
Will you let the leader
Bring out the leader in you, too?

Do you have the vision
To see the possible become the reality?
Do you have the vision
To see change happen in your lifetime?

Do you have the vision
To be a part of the solution and not the problem?
Do you have the vision to see
How to make things better for yourself and others?

Renovate.
Educate.
Contemplate.
Motivate.
Stimulate.
It's not too late to be a part of the vision!

THE MELODIES OF CHRISTMAS ('TIS THE SEASON)

(Sing) "'Tis the Season to be Jolly"
To be thankful for the roof over our heads,
To be thankful for the food on our tables,
And to be thankful for the jobs we sometime hate.
'Tis the season to remember –
The Shut-Ins, The Elderly,
The Lonely,
Those dying from AIDS and CANCER
Remember --
The women and children
Being abused and murdered across the land.

(Sing) "Chestnuts Roasting on an Open Fire"
Have been replaced by the hands of homeless men,
Women, and children warming themselves.
Sadly, Jack Frost
Is more than a casual acquaintance,
And he is no longer considered kind.

(Sing) "Let it snow, let it snow, let it snow",
But bring these homeless indoors.
(Sing) "I'm Dreaming of a White Christmas,"
A Black, Yellow, Brown, and Red Christmas,
A world full of peace –
Where people find value in their differences,
Tolerance instead of bigotry,
Respect for those they feel they are unable to love.
(Sing) "Have Yourself a Merry Little Christmas"
Have a life full of good health.
Have a family that loves you.
Have success in your every endeavor.
Have the Prince of Peace as your constant companion.
That's the best Christmas present of all!
(Sing) Hallelujah! Hallelujah!

THANK YOU, HEAVENLY FATHER

Thank you, Heavenly Father for making all things possible.
Thank you for keeping me safe, and
healthy enough for the task.
Thank you for keeping me in my right mind.

Thank you for giving me the strength and fortitude
to be a testimony to
Your Unconditional Love,
Grace,
Mercy,
and
Favor.

Patricia Ann Woolfork

The Measure of a Man Is in His Name

Principled, progressive, prevailing, prayerful, and powerful
Affable, authoritative, and awesome
Sincere, sensational, and sympathetic
Tender, tenacious, timely – tell it like it is teacher, thankful
Observant, opinionated, open and original
Resourceful, respected and real down to earth

Object of our affection and respect

Worshipful, willing, and wonderful
Emotionally engaged and empathetic
Navigator of ministries and members
Daring and dutiful
Ever in the seeking of the presence of God, endearing
Loving, learned and loyal
Leader with vision

Dedicated, determined
Appreciative, affectionate
Virtuous, vital
Inspired and inspirational, informative and instructive
Shepherd, sanctified, and set apart to be a servant of the Lord

Pastor's 25th Anniversary, May 2014
Union Chapel Missionary Baptist Church,
Huntsville, Alabama

WHAT IS A PASTOR?

A pastor is someone who is, first and foremost, a

Preacher of God's Word, a Praise Maker, and Practices Patience
Accessible, Approachable, an Advisor
Sincere, a Shepherd
Teacher, Trustworthy, Truthful
Original
Resourceful and Respected.

A pastor should be and is

Memorable in his teaching and his Musicality
Intelligent, Inspiring
Loving, Loyal
Tenacious in Tending to the flock, Talented
Open-minded, but Spirit led, and Optimistic – a
Natural born leader

Our pastor is

Benevolent and Big-Hearted
Imaginative, Interesting, and full of Integrity
Gracious, Generous
Giving – Oh, don't forget how Good-looking he says he is!
Honest, Humorous, Hopeful
Admirable, Appreci*ated, Awesome,*
Motivating, Moving, Mesmerizing, Musical – a Man of God!

Well done, good and faithful servant on your
18th Anniversary, June 5, 2011
Mount Vernon Missionary Baptist, Newark, NJ

Patricia Ann Woolfork

THERE'S NO PLACE LIKE HOME

"There's no place like home."
I didn't realize how true this was
Until I left my church and home for six months.
Although I visited many churches in my absence,
Heard dynamic sermons,
I learned, "There's no place like home."

Though songs were sung,
They weren't The Voices from the Mount,
Brother Malloy or Pastor Biggham.
Rarely was I moved to stomp and shout and cry
As I am moved in that place.
No one can make a more joyful noise
Than Brother Perry and his posse'.
"There's no place like home."

"There's no place like home."
I missed the good hugs, smiling faces,
And genuine affection.
I missed the food served by the Manna Ministry.
Those sisters know how to put their feet in a pot!
I really missed Sister Leggett's Jell-O Cake!

I was adopted by a tiny church
In the beautiful countryside of Boyds, Maryland.
The people at St. Mark's were friendly and hospitable,
But most were resistant to change –
Too bogged down in religiosity and ritual
To be affected by Word based sermons –

Unwilling to participate, volunteer,
Go to choir rehearsal,
Attend Bible Study, or even be joyous in their worship
Although the Pastor was spirit-filled and enthusiastic.
"There's no place like home."

Savoring Eden

There is no Pastor like Rev, Dr. Milton Biggham,
And he has a pretty good back up crew, too!
Thank you for your
Diligence,
Preparation, and
Good Shepherding.

God's Spirit is in this place.
You can feel it.
It is so permeating
That I can hardly wait to get there
To have it poured out upon me!
It's in the music and song,
The fellowship, the teaching.
It's in the prayer and praise.

It is a privilege that we should never take for granted.
We are blessed
And some of us don't even know it or care –
Just taking up space!

Like every family, we have a few black sheep,
But God loves each and every one of us.
We are works in progress,
But look how far some of us have already come!
It's like the parable about the talents. . . (Luke 19:11-27)
We can lose what we have
If we don't appreciate it or utilize it.
Change and growth are good things.
Knowledge is power, and
Encouragement is contagious.
God is able, and
"There's no place like home."

Dedicated to Mount Vernon Missionary Baptist Church,
Newark, NJ – November 2006

THE PERFECT CHEER!

Two, four, six, eight
Who do we appreciate?
Our Father, the Creator of all things!
Creatures great and small,
The earth, the sun, moon, and stars,
The very air we breathe,
The Creator of sight and sound,
Wind and rain, and
Sand and seas.

Two, four, six, eight
What do we appreciate?
All that God has blessed us with –
Our children, our parents, our friends,
The roof over our heads,
The food on our table –
Even the job we complain about, or
The job we are waiting for.

Two, four, six, eight
What should we appreciate?
Each day we wake up to new possibilities,
Every breath we take
Because they should not be taken for granted,
Our hair, even if it is grey –
Just because He graced us to live long enough,
To see the change!
Our bodies – short, tall, thin or fat,
Because He loves us just the way we are!
We are all of His children, and
He provides for us as all good Fathers do.

Savoring Eden

Two, four, six, eight
How can we show that we appreciate?
Be tolerant and patient with each other.
Be thankful for everything,
Help others less fortunate,
Be a blessing to someone,
Believe without complaint, even in the down times,
That He is faithful to His promises
To return beauty for ashes and abundance
Instead of lack.

Two, four, six, eight
What can I appreciate?
He has given me a gift, and
I must use it or lose it!
My best is just around the corner.
I am the creator of my own circumstances.
I am to be directed by my Creator in all things.
I am alive, creative, strong and courageous.
I have friends and family that love me,
I have left a mark on time and space.

Patricia Ann Woolfork

WORDS TO PJ FOR HIGH SCHOOL GRADUATION

My dearest grandson,

Your 18th birthday was a major milestone in your young life.
However, today is the beginning of your future.
What you do from this day forward
Will impact upon everything you do.
You have an opportunity before you that few have
Either had an opportunity to embark upon or
Not enough sense to take the advantage – EDUCATION!

Surround yourself with people of like mind and
The desire to succeed and advance.
Don't blow your life goals
For friends, associates, or even family.
Your future is in your hands.
You alone are responsible for it.

Remain focused – STUDY!
Make life-long friends.
Love yourself.
Trust yourself.
Trust the knowledge of your elders
To guide you on the right path.
INVITE God into your life.
HE created you with a PLAN.

You make us proud each day you take a breath.
Learn from the mistakes that others your age
Have made in the past.
Be assured that you are LOVED.
You are FAVORED.
You are SPECIAL.

The next chapter will be full of challenges.
Face them like the young man I know you can be.

Be my first College Graduate!
I plan to be here to see it
If God allows me to be there for the event.
But whether I am or not,
I will be there in spirit and hopefully in your heart.
Do not disappoint either me or yourself!

Remember . . . .
You promised to look after me when I get older.
You will need a GOOD JOB to keep that promise!

Smiling and loving you more each day,

Nannu

HAPPY 18TH BIRTHDAY, PJ

Happy 18th Birthday, PJ
You will become an adult between 2:30 – 3:30 p.m. today.
I am most blessed to have been there to be the first to greet you and hold you and place you in your mother's arms. What a happy day!

Although you will have some maturing to do as you navigate this maze we call "life," I am confident in your inherent ability to make the wise decisions necessary for you to become the man God created you to be in order to bring Him glory and honor!

In three years you will be considered a full-grown man in nearly every society around the globe. The choices you make from now on will affect most of your future endeavors. You alone will be responsible and held accountable for those choices. Consider the advice given by your parents and your Nannu as guidelines because we have already been where you are going, made mistakes we want to spare you from repeating, know the consequences of not listening to that inner voice or gut that warns us that we are about to mess up, but go ahead and do it anyway, etc. I guess what I am trying to say is that we have your back, and we love you and there is nothing you can do about it!

Have we made mistakes, said the wrong thing, pissed you off, disappointed you? YES! They did not give us an owner's manual or "how to" book on January 20, 1995. We did get a heart full of love and good intention, equipped with doing only the best we knew how to do to provide you with all that you needed to have a good foundation for a successful outcome.
BELIEVE THAT!   XOXO

Your loving grandmother,

Nannu

HAPPY 20TH BIRTHDAY, PJ

Have an awesome 20th birthday grandson!
You are very much loved.
I will forever cherish my memory of this day.
I was the first family to hold you.
I am so grateful to be your grandmother.
I am proud of you.
How time has flown!

On today,
Reflect on all of the things you can do
To prepare a path for a life full of
Success,
Fulfillment,
Good Health, and
Happiness
From this day forward.
Your future is really up to you!

Patricia Ann Woolfork

A Birthday Moment

Today is my grandson's 21st birthday.
How time flies!
Twenty-one years ago, around 3:00 p.m.,
I watched his birth, and after he was wrapped up,
I got to hand him to my daughter.
What a privilege to be the first of his family
To lay hands on him.
It took over twenty-three hours for him to arrive –
All of us tired and excited.

Now I get to celebrate
Another milestone in his life – Adulthood.
We have had many times to be proud.
He was an extraordinary athlete,
Proficient in both basketball and football
Even getting recognition as
"Player of the Week" in the news.
He is currently attending A& M University,
And taking his education more seriously.

Among his many talents,
He is a budding vocalist and songwriter.
Most of all, he is funny, sensitive, loving,
Intelligent, ridiculously goofy, and handsome!
But, of course, I am biased.
I am his Nannu!

Have an awesome day.
Be wise, careful and stay safe.
Remember how much I love you and
How much you mean to me.
I am counting on you to continue
To make me even prouder,
If that is even possible.

I Could Not Wait to Tell You

I woke up with thoughts of you so vivid
That I heard the sound of your voice
Piercing through the cobwebs in my brain.
My next coherent thought embodied the
Vision and recollection of the warrior woman
You embody in the petite form of yours.

I was so moved by it that I had to
Prop these heavy eyelids open,
Find your number, and
Through clouded, allergy-filled vision
Type this message to you to let you know
How profoundly grateful I am
For the privilege of meeting you and learning about
Your incredible tenacity and wit, and
Having the honor of calling you "friend."

I know all is well with you because I know
You are in the protective care of
Our Father's loving hands and grace.

We so seldom get to tell each other
How important our interactions are,
No matter how brief, but
Branded in our spirits and hearts
To pop up in unsolicited times such as this.

Be well my little sister/daughter.
I just wanted to let you know
That thoughts and fondness of you
Woke me this morning, and
I, would not, and
Could not wait to tell you.

Dedicated to Regina

Patricia Ann Woolfork

HAPPY 15TH BIRTHDAY, KRISTEN

I can hardly believe that 15 years have passed
since I witnessed your birth and handed you to your mom.
My little pink bunny has blossomed
into a stunning young woman
with multitudes of potential and talents.

You are a gift from God.
He has given you another year
to reflect upon your mistakes,
renew your resolve
to be the best
daughter, sister, friend,
example, student, and
entrepreneur you can become.

He has given you time
to use the intelligence He has given you
to make better decisions about your conduct,
your choice of relationships,
the Kristen you want to present
to your peers and educators.
He has given you time to
change your attitudes toward others,
become both empathetic,
sympathetic and respectful toward others.
With each new year,
you become more accountable
for your own actions, decisions, and
the consequences of same.
Be your own best friend.
Defend your future like no one else can.
Colleges and employers look at social media.
What you post and who you associate with
can derail your dreams faster than anything.
Teach yourself to be
more kind and less judgmental.

Savoring Eden

Love yourself with more intensity
than you look for it from others (especially males).

You have been bestowed
with beauty, brains, creativity and talent.
Make them work for you
in a way that makes God smile, and
continue to pour his Grace upon you.
Remember . . .
He will never leave you.
He will lift you up
when you are feeling down or disappointed.

I am so blessed that
He chose me to be your grandmother.
It is the best gift he has given us.
Let's continue to unwrap it together.
Happy 15th Birthday!
Enjoy it with gratitude.

Love, Nannu,
2018

The Start of Something Big

What a happy feeling to be a mother.
First one child and then another.
Soon the sister has a brother.
Solve one problem,
Boom!
Another.

Your grateful heart finds joy
If it's a baby boy.
You're simply out of this world
To learn you've had a girl.

The diapers and the pins,
The trouble just begins.
Your husband says, "That's fine,"
And you have lost your mind!
The babies cry.
The bottles break.
And, oh! Your back,
What an ache!
You haven't had much sleep
For the ghastly hours that you keep.

The booties and the blankets,
The carriers and the cribs,
The pacifiers and the nightshirts,
Gowns, bottles, and bibs!

But, all in all
As your figure falls,
You know you can't escape it.
You're a Mommy now
And how!
So stand up and take your bow!

1970

TO MY FIRSTBORN CHILD, RUSSELL

I am so proud to be your mother.
Your birth gave my life purpose in so many ways.
I hope this new year of life
Brings you the happiness and success you seek.

I ask that God keeps you both safe and in good health.
I am asking Him to keep me around
To wish you many more birthday blessings.

I love your creativity,
Your multiple talents,
Your big, loving heart,
Your tenderness and strength, and
Your unconditional love for me.

I love you dearly, my firstborn child, and
There is nothing you can do about it.
XOXOXOXO

Patricia Ann Woolfork

ROAD TRIP PART I

Dawn was about to break
As we started our trip out of Huntsville
Toward Highway 72 E for the three hundred odd miles toward
Somewhere called Kingsport in nearby Tennessee,
Our rental car appearing to be
The lone traveler on the darkened roadway
With only moonlight, like a light house beacon,
To show us the way until the headlights
Landed upon the embedded reflectors in the pavement.

"Not a creature was stirring,
Not even a mouse,"
Except for the three of us girls
Three generations
Together, at last,
For our first ever all girl road trip.

It seemed as though the whole world was asleep
Like my granddaughter on the back seat.
The store lights were off and
Only their signs made us aware of their presence –
Together with the string lights which hung over car lots
Swinging in the already sweltering Alabama breeze.

Occasionally we were met by another traveler
Who meandered through a blinking traffic light
To join us for a few miles
So we could follow each other's tail lights
And play catch up and pass
To avoid the boredom and tedium of a pre-dawn trek
Without caffeine and not enough sleep.

Yawning is the tune played for many a mile
When nearly alone on an open road
And there is no CD player,

Savoring Eden

And the radio stations keep going in and out of reception
Through the hills and dales of this stretch of highway –
Unless you like "hillbilly."

Cognizance resurfaces
When passing an open gas station or convenience store or
When coming across an interesting billboard or
The highway sign which read, "Get Hammered, Get Nailed."
Newly displayed for the long holiday weekend.

Then you glance at the speedometer –
Look for a trooper –
Proceed with caution –
Grateful for the escape, this time –
Until zombie-like,
You get back in that zone and
Catch yourself –
Swearing it won't happen again.

When suddenly,
Your side seat navigator,
Who has been nearly comatose the whole time,
Is awakened by the motion which comes
After coming out of a steep curve
Tells you,
"It's your ticket."

Patricia Ann Woolfork

HAPPY BIRTHDAY TO MY DAUGHTER

You have made it to another year of life
Through God's continued Grace.
Do your best to show Him
How much gratitude you have for this Gift.
Continue to grow in humility, compassion,
Patience, empathy, love, generosity,
Selflessness, and forgiveness of self and others.
You have the capacity and the intelligence
To make all challenges become victories,
If you push yourself out of your own way.

As your mom, of course,
I want only the best for you.
I am proud of your accomplishments, thus far,
In these xxxx+ years –
Professionally, Educationally,
Financially, and personally but,
We all have to continue to be better –
Not become complacent,
Bogged down
In our own self-interests.

We only look in a rearview mirror
To catch a glance
At what is behind us, or might be approaching
So we can safely make a move.
But, most of our attention is drawn to looking ahead
To see what's coming in front of our path.
That is why the windshield
Is bigger than the rearview mirror –
Things recede as we move further forward.

This is my birthday wish for you today:
Be happy.
Be brave – slay those remaining giants.

Be the best wife, mother, sister, aunt, friend,
Daughter and person you were born to be!

HE knew you by the hairs on your head
Before you were born.
HE knew what your abilities would be, and
How you would turn out.
HE has even given you the tools
To accomplish All Things for HIS Glory.
HE has even given you the Time.
You awoke to another Birthday.
This is a gift not given to those we have lost.
So make this the best birthday ever.

December 29th – the day God gifted you to me.
    "This is the day the Lord hath made.
    Rejoice and be glad in it!"

Patricia Ann Woolfork

MY AMERICA

If we were founded on Christian principles, explain:
400 years of slavery, genocide, and
Displacement and slaughter of the Native Americans,
Burning suspected "witches,"
Lynching of Black men and women,
Segregation, denying the right to vote,
Unequal education, unequal pay,
Racism, and bigotry,
Internment of American citizens,
Vietnam and Iraq,
Unequal justice or lack thereof of justice,
Intolerance,
Distortion of history . . .
Need I go on?

This nation was founded by people
Fleeing from religious persecution themselves,
Who then tried to impose their beliefs on others –
People who came from a class-based country
Then looked down their noses on people
They felt were beneath them.
This nation was founded by Treaty and promise breakers –
Liars,
Murderers, and Thieves.

The Bible teaches
Honesty, loyalty,
Love, unselfishness,
Patience, kindness,
The Golden Rule:
Do unto others as you would have done to yourself.
It teaches
Charity, and purity in thought and deed.
So where are these Christian principles of which we speak?

Savoring Eden

Just because our currency says "In God We Trust,"
Does not a Christian principle make!
This nation was forged on the principle of
Liberty and justice for all,
Freedom of speech and religion
"All men/women are created equal."

This is what is missing in America.
Until we make these things a reality for all Americans –
The rich and the poor,
People of all races, denominations, genders and sexualities,
WE will never be a nation built on any kind of principle.

GOD must have a place in our nation,
But whose god/God
Is a freedom of choice –
To be treated with respect and reverence.
Most people, no matter the way they worship,
Are taught to love their neighbors,
Take care of their families,
Work hard,
Do well,
Praise and worship, and
Give to the less fortunate, etc.

It is time for all of us to do our individual parts
To make this the land of promise again and
Stop pointing fingers and take responsibility –
Make reparations for our past transgressions, and
Let go of the learned hatred and divisions among us.
      Life is too short to do otherwise.

Patricia Ann Woolfork

I Cry When . . .

I watch a movie about my history of which I know so little –
    The struggle for survival waged by my people
        Betrayed by their leaders
            Sold into slavery for financial gain
    Lost at sea in masse
        Because of disease, filth, and over-crowding
        Thrown overboard for recreation
        Raped in front of their men and children.
I cry when . . .
    I revisit a re-enactment of the Civil Rights Movement –
        As I see my people beaten across their backs,
        Their heads with clubs, pipes, and bats
        Attacked by dogs and water hoses, and
        Shot while protecting their elders from harm.
I cry when. . .
    I see politicians use us as pawns for power and
        Convenience to promote their agenda –
As they perpetuate an untruth of perceived inequality
        While they portray us all as parasites,
        Welfare Queens, beasts and thugs
        While we have been denied equal education
        Equal protection under the law
        Equal pay
        Equal housing
        Equity in paying taxes, etc., etc.
I cry when . . .
    Despite all the pseudo-opportunities and
        Inequitable advancements –
    Most of our young men, our future leaders and fathers,
        Have no connection with our past,
Still have low self-esteem
        Aspire to nothing other than
            Becoming the next superstar athlete or rapper

Savoring Eden

Still call each other "Nigger"
        Call their women "bitches" and "hoes"
        Wear their pants below their asses
        Are no longer chivalrous, industrious, or respectful
While many of our young women act out in kind
        Find this bad behavior acceptable
        Demean themselves
        While baring their breasts and behinds
        Acting more like hookers and sluts
        Instead of using their brains
        To become future leaders, wives, and mothers.

        We are the progeny of kings and queens
              – not court jesters –
        We dishonor their sacrifice and their memories,

I cry when . . .
        I observe the blatant disrespect heaped upon
        Our first President of Color.
        He has been called "devil"
        Fellow statesmen have called him "liar"
        He has been defied at every turn.
        His programs has been halted by filibuster,
        Et cetera,
              Et cetera,
                      Et cetera.

GUESS WHAT MY SON TOLD ME

"I love My Mother so very much.
There's not a day that goes by,
That a lesson learned from her doesn't manifest its self.

The decent and honorable man I am today,
Is because of the Grace of ALLAH
And my beautiful Mother –
A Survivor,
Loving,
Strong, and
Wise.

I am blessed EVERY DAY
That HE,
The Most Gracious,
The Most Merciful,
Chose
YOU to be MY MOTHER!"

Happy Mother's Day!
May 11, 2014

SENTIMENTS FOR THE NEW YEAR

We smiled.
We laughed.
We argued, and
We probably even disagreed on things,
But through it all I love you!

I can't imagine going through the New Year
Without you.
Take this moment . . . .
To let family and friends know that you love them
Because you never know when that day might come
That it will be too late.
Send this to everyone you love.
I just did.

May each and every one of you
Find joy and peace in the coming New Year.
Hold on tightly to those you call friends
Because they are hard to come by.

Love those that are your family,
Not just because you are supposed to,
But....unconditionally!

Life is work . . .
Do it with full dedication and pride –
Having the best life possible!

Love to you all

MOTHERS

Celebrate all mothers for the gift they gave us – Life.
It is the greatest job,
The most thankless job,
The lowest paid job,
The never-ending job,
The job with the longest job description
With no "on the job" training.
There are no vacations, sick days, or holidays.

We love you with every beat of our hearts, but
Sometimes we don't like you very much,
If the truth be told.

We are often misunderstood,
Under appreciated,
Disrespected,
And feel unloved, but
We never put in our resignation papers –
It is 'til death do us part – even if from afar.

There were no training manuals
So we had to figure it out.
Sometimes we got it right, but more often than not,
It was hit or miss.
It was our best most of the time, or
The best we were capable of doing.

That is why we should celebrate our mothers –
Especially those that stuck it out until
We could care for ourselves.
Celebrate those who knew their limitations and
Surrendered us to more capable, "want to be" mothers.

If you still have your mother,
Cherish the privilege.
She won't be around always.
If you have lost your mother,
Cherish the good memories of her.
If you are yet to become a mother,
Consider it a privilege and an honor –
Some women would kill to be able to do so.

Celebrate who you have become –
Because of your mother.
Whether you love her or hate her,
You carry parts of her in your DNA –
An inescapable fact.
Try to right the wrongs with your own offspring
And Forgive
Your mother
Unconditionally...
Leave the past in the past.
Your heart will be less heavy.
Today is another chance to get it right.

To all the mothers we lost.
We miss you!
God bless you all.

I Get to Rant, Too

I just want to comment on all the venomous talk against President Obama's address last night. As for the candidates running, especially those with no political experience – how do you even know what you would do in the same situation if you never had to make the same said decision?

To the other pessimists: Have you ever pondered the thought that a president, with any common sense, would not broadcast on international media what his next action would be to the enemy? Maybe he is appearing to be unforthcoming as a tactic to keep the enemy thinking that there would be no retribution for their actions – lulling them into a false sense of security. President Obama is an intelligent, thinking man who does not reveal his cards to his opponents.

What the American people should be doing is force Congress to pass a law banning the sale of assault weapons to any private citizen. That does not negate the right to bear arms. How much armor does one need? A hand gun for protection that does not use a magazine of multiple bullets and a rifle for hunting which should also not be rapid firing should be enough for any one person.

And now for my final rant: After all the criticism, name calling, ie. Devil, liar, etc, — I am glad that President Obama has displayed the most suave, intelligent, cool, down-to-earth image to the American people.

He has been a perfect example of a husband who loves his wife and a father who loves his children. Mrs. Obama is also a class act—admired around the globe. Their children have not been the object of bad press. There have been no stories about infidelity, as with other presidents.

I wish I could be more like Mr. Obama. He is of African descent, as am I, but he is able to maintain his cool despite the overt and covert racism perpetrated against him. They cannot take away his legacy as the first President of color, not once, but two consecutive terms.

My hope is that when he leaves the White House, no pun intended, he will write a tell-all book about his journey and the dedication should read: "To all the haters and non-supporters: "Suck My Dick." Being of African descent, it should be big enough for them to choke on.

Yes, I said it! "Kiss my ass!" just didn't feel right to me. And, if you don't like what I have said in this post, you know what you can do!

RANT II

No matter what the haters say or do,
President Obama is an awesome individual.
He is a class act,
He is a role model for our Black young men.
He is super intelligent,
He is cool under fire,
He is a great husband and father,
He is down-to-earth, and
He still knows from whence he came.

He got handed a mess
When he entered the office, but
He has done his best in the face of
Blatant disrespect of his position and
The attempted assassination of his character,
He still did not stoop down to their level –
He was able to keep
"Them in Their Place"
With dignity and finesse.

He oozes swagger and coolness,
He can carry a tune and bust a move!
He is not afraid
To show how much he loves his wife and children –
Yet another role model for our sons, brothers ,and fathers.

I don't know what the history books will say
about his two terms in office,- they have left out truth and facts
before, but they will be unable to erase his legacy
of being the first Black – true African American
President of these **United** States.
 (Really?)
I pray for his continued health and safety, and
I wish him peace and blessings when his term is over.

HAPPY NEW YEAR 2011

My resolve this New Year's Day, 2011;
Take care of Patricia Ann Woolfork!
Be open to greatness, prosperity, happiness,
Good health, and friendship –
Even love from all the right places.

Learn from my past and not repeat it.
Move on from toxic relationships.
Don't expect reciprocity, and
I will not be disappointed.
Be resolved to love myself without hang-ups,
Reservations, conditions, or guilt.
Get out of my own way!

In all things, listen to that inner voice –
Don't ignore it ever again!
Be safe.
Be vigilante for opportunities for success.
Embrace them not run away from them.
Do my best and be my best
In all my life challenges and relationships.

Accept what I cannot change.
Do not change my core personality.
She is a good person –
I am good.
I am worthy.
I am beautiful.
I am loving.
I am giving.
I am loveable.
I am God's reflection.
I have only just begun to turn my life around.
Look out – here I come!

Patricia Ann Woolfork

A DREAM REVISITED

We are born, grow old, and then die.
The time in between is spent in pursuit of our dreams.
The time remaining is left to enjoy the fruit of our labors.

We continue our race by building a family.
We secure our future by making a home.
We struggle in youth for a reward in our later years.
We make sacrifices in our prime
So that old age can be secure.
We build our life on dreams,
Yet our sorrows are built on reality.

In my youth,
I carried my bride over an imaginary threshold,
And our children were born in a home not our own.
However,
My dream stayed alive and that home became mine.

My dream has not become bitter –
Even though my house is no longer my home,
And I cannot sit under my "vine" or "fig tree"
Because they have been uprooted.

I have yet another dream –
That God will make a way
For us to be reunited with hearth and home
Before our golden years dwindle away,
While there is still time to enjoy the fruit of our toil, and
Have a taste of the "good life," and in this dream,
The threshold is mine again to share with my loving wife.

Dedicated to the families in Montclair, NJ that were displaced due to Radon Gas, and to some who never got to go back home.

EARTH REVISITED

The whispering, haunting wind
Blew the sheer curtain aside,
And the edge of the world lay exposed.
Cold as the steel of a razor,
Naked as a clock without hands,
The silence was deafening
At the edge of the world.

THOSE WERE THE GOOD OLD DAYS

We stayed outside until the street lights came on.
We rode our bikes, jumped rope, played kickball and hopscotch.
We got scrapes and cuts.
We got hosed with iodine and mercurochrome.
We were obedient to our parents.
We didn't talk back even if we knew or thought they were wrong.
We had chores to do.
We had to earn our allowance.
We had to do our best in school or suffer the consequences.
We'd rather die than get detention after school.
We said prayers in school regardless of religious denomination.
We showed respect to our teachers and administrators.
We went to school to learn.
We were disciplined, but we learned to accept the rules.
We asked permission to speak when grown-ups were talking.
We had to say yes/no mam and yes/no sir to our elders.
We did everything as a family.
We ate our meals together.
We ate what was put in front of us or nothing at all.
We said grace.
We said our prayers before bed.
We turned the TV off.
We had real conversations with each other.
We read and studied scriptures and worshipped together.
We did not know what "dysfunctional" meant.
We had music that meant something.
We still hear it being heard today.
We had good, clean fun.
We made life-long friends.
We had pride even if we had little.
We respected ourselves and others.
We took advantage of opportunities offered to us.
We became contributing members to society.
Those were the good old days.

MY OBSERVATION OF A MAN OF CHARACTER

J OVIAL, JOCOSE, JOCULAR, JESTER, JUDICIOUS, JUBILANT, JAUNTY

O UTGOING, OBSERVANT, OPEN-HEARTED, OUTSTANDING, ORIGINAL

H ONEST, HARD-WORKING, HEARTWARMING, HILARIOUS, HONORABLE

N ICE, NECESSARY, NATURAL, NATTY, NEEDED

E. NTHUSIASTIC, ENJOYABLE, EMPATHETIC, ENCOURAGING, EXUBERANT

C REATIVE, CONVIVIAL, CARING, CURIOUS, COMPASSIONATE, CHEERFUL

A UTHENTIC, AMAZING, ADVENTUROUS, AMUSING, AMIABLE, ANIMATED

R ESOURSEFUL, REFLECTIVE, RELIABLE, RESPONSIVE, RESPECTED

S INCERE, SELF-DISCIPLINED, STIRRING, STIMULATING

O PTIMISTIC, OBLIGING, OPINIONATED, OTHER-WORLDLY

N OTEWORTHY, NOVEL, NEAT, NURTURING

Captain, My Captain, HAPPY BIRTHDAY, 2018!

MY GRANDSON IS . . .

. . .
. . . Quietly introspective
. . . Smart and coy
. . . An exceptional athlete
. . . An awesome team player
. . . Friendly and loyal
. . . Steady and easy-going
. . . Contemplative and calculating
. . . Soft spoken and unassuming
. . . Affectionate
. . . Endearing and gregarious
. . . Confidant and self-reliant
. . . A smooth operator
. . . Handsome and fashionable
. . . A little brother
. . . A big brother
. . . A ferocious protector
. . . The best movie watching buddy
. . . An independent spirit
. . . Hot sauce loving
. . . My blue-eyed wonder boy
. . . Jalen Xavier

I am so very proud of you. You give the best unsolicited hugs.

My Daughter from Another Mother

She is my diamond in the rough, and priceless nonetheless.
She has a heart of gold and is full of kindness and generosity.
She is nurturing and affectionate.
She is fun loving.
She is a go-getter.
She is a great caregiver.
She is humble and full of gratitude.
She is eager to learn and a diehard student.
She is full of self-confidence, but humble.
She is loyal and trustworthy.
She is an overcomer of many childhood adversities.
She is a great mother and loving wife.
She is God-fearing and faithful.
She is strong and outspoken when necessary.
She is a protector – a gladiator for the weak.
She is an exceptional cook and keeper of my traditional meals.
She is someone I watched blossom into a beautiful woman.
She was the bearer of my first grandchild, who has blessed me
 with my first great-grandchild.
She is my daughter, whose real mother also shared my name.
She was a dutiful and loving daughter right to the end.
She is a beautiful spirit.
She loves me just the way I am and just because.
She is my unconditional friend and forever family.
She is my daughter from another mother,
 Tracey Denise.

Journey in Search of Self

JOURNEY IN SEARCH OF SELF

This portion of the book addresses some of the pitfalls that occur to a child or an adult that has been traumatized. It addresses the emotional and psychological ideations that often come from it. When a child is betrayed by a parent, it is difficult for them to enter into safe relationships later in life. We often become people pleasers and enablers just trying to fill a void, or because we feel unworthy of anything better. We suffer from both shame and guilt.

Unfortunately, there are periods of deep depression and loneliness, looking for love in all the wrong places, repeated disappointment, and attempts to end one's life—usually because of an additional trauma in adulthood. Fortunately, I was able to get help to learn coping skills that did not result in addiction.

Writing became my venting tool and my life preserver. It allowed me to pour out my heart, release the floodgates of tears, and see hope on the other side. It gets better, but you have work to do.

These are explanations and confrontations, and inspiring pieces as well. Perhaps you will see something that you can relate to and be encouraged that you are not alone. We are more alike than we are different.

Maybe this does not apply to you personally, but I bet you know someone who could be encouraged that there is light at the end of the tunnel. All you have to do is look for it.

Explanations, Confrontations, and Reflections

TURBULENCE

There is turbulence within me
Tossing me back and forth from fantasy into reality,
Denying my dreams
Stripping away my desires;
Telling me over and over again
That I do not deserve.
Teasing me with overtures of delight,
Telling me, "Yes you can,"
Then snatching my positivity away.

If only I could remain constant –
Find joy for longer than a moment,
Security for more than an hour,
A lover for more than a day,
Love for a lifetime.

I am full of love and empathy.
I am generous
in my willingness to be of service to others.

I am adventurous and open-minded.
I am always seeking ways to be further enlightened.
I am ever searching for ways
to improve my character and personality.

I am an ever-evolving creation of God.
Loved just the way I am.
I am a true reflection
of His ever-enduring love
 – just because.

CONTEMPLATION

Sometimes I struggle
to find the words
that will draw a picture
of what my thoughts and
feeling convey.
I face a never-ending battle
with feelings of inadequacy and
irrelevance which often consume
my, too infrequent, thoughts
of being unique, gifted, talented,
interesting, and intellectual.

I have accomplished
a great deal despite my past.
But why is it that the negative
always seem to beat the hell out of
the positive experiences in my life?

I wish I knew how to turn off
the misinformation that
was mapped onto my brain as a child,
that taught me to believe
what I was told about myself
as I developed into adulthood –
even though time and again,
I have had irrefutable proof
that my parents were wrong.

How can I erase those memories,
once and for all, so that the floodgates
of my creativity will be fully opened
and free-flowing without hesitation,
disbelief, or incredulity as to its truth,
relevance or value?
How do I stop the need for validation?
I am an intelligent person.

This is not rocket science.
I can do this.
It is not too late
to make a change of my total self!
I CAN DO IT
If not now, when?

Patricia Ann Woolfork

MY LETTER OF APOLOGIES

To all that it may concern:

I have spent most of my life trying to make up for my insecurities and short-comings. I've tried buying my friends. I've tried denying myself, doing for others instead of myself, only to be kicked repeatedly. I feel that my "best" has never and will never be good enough to please anyone.

To my children: I am sorry for all the mistakes I made trying to raise you by myself. I tried to be the best mother I knew how to be. I tried to give you all the love I felt that I never received. My one regret is that I tried to be your "friend" instead of your parent. I indulged you, I spoiled you, and I probably even screwed you up emotionally. What did I have to work with?

I came from a home that was loveless. I came from abusive parents whether it was physical, emotional, or sexual in nature. It was still abuse. I had nothing to compare what true love really was or is. I've been searching for it my entire life—a hopeless endeavor. I've looked for it in all the wrong places with all the wrong people. Never knowing what my true value was, I exploited myself in order to fill a void, to make ends meet, to give you things I thought you deserved. Did that make me a whore? Maybe so. I didn't see it that way at the time.

What did you really go lacking for? You always had a nice home, good food, an allowance, toys, outings to the movies, roller skating, etc. Yes, you also had to endure my bouts with depression and hospitalizations. I am sorry for all of that. There were so many times that I thought if I ended my life, you would be better off. And now, at this stage of my life—I find that not much has changed in that area.

I have spent countless years trying to erase the damage some of my actions or inactions have caused. I am sorry I was unable to protect you or that I was even unaware that I needed to protect you from certain things, especially my father. For that I am deeply sorry. Had I not had this pathological tendency to trust people, maybe you could have been spared.

I feel that I have failed you and myself. But no matter what my feelings are, I loved you and I always wanted you. It pains me now that I can be so easily cast aside because of my failure to be perfect or my inability to meet your expectations. I respect your anger. What I don't respect is your lack of respect. Maybe I couldn't do my best—but you at least made it to adulthood without becoming addicts or jailbirds! You got a decent education. You were exposed to the arts and music.

To my daughter: I was there for you every time you needed me. I was there for each pregnancy, each birth—each time a baby came home, I was the one to help you take care of it. Every time you got sick, it was me who left work or my own home to take care of you and your family. So you are upset that you offered to pay me and I accepted it—had my finances been better, and often times they were, I would have gladly done it for free. I thought that we were just helping each other.

But now you want me to lose your phone number. You don't want to be a part of my life and I suppose that means my grand-children as well. I will respect your wishes however much it pains me to do so. And for the last time, I am sorry that my father molested you. I hope that you will find a way to get pass the trauma and take responsibility for your own life and how it's turned out. Everything is not my fault!

Who packed up your belongings each and every time you moved? Who unpacked and set up your home every place you moved? Who took care of your children when they were sick and you needed to work? Who slept in a chair in a hospital room when Kristen almost died? Who stayed with you after surgeries and infections, etc.? Who cooked and cleaned and washed your laundry, picked up your kids or delivered them to school? Who other than yourself and your husband dared to love them more than me?

I wish I could say the same about myself. I have a mother who doesn't call or write. I was never wanted nor needed. A "responsibility" is what my mother called me. And now I have a daughter who neither loves me or respects me—one who says that I eat too much of her food and use too much of her utilities—a daughter who asks me on the day I get out of the hospital, "how soon are you leaving?" I have a daughter who gives gifts and takes them away—a daughter who doesn't keep her word or her own arrangements.

Yes, I have made many mistakes not the least of which was nip all of this in the bud when you were a child. I should have demanded your respect not wished for it. I wanted so much not to be like my own mother that I ruined you. You seem to want to hurt me every chance that you get. Then you wonder why I become defensive. I have finally grown tired—I am too old to fight against the inevitable. Just know that I have never stopped loving you. I may not like certain things about you, but I still love you!

To my middle son: Wherever you are—I don't know why you left me out of your life. Your sister says it's because you said that I was a whore. My cousin says that she was told it was because I molested you (which I never did!), but she got that tidbit from your grandfather's sister, Julia. We all know that he was a lying, perverted, sick motherfucker who didn't die soon enough! But to you: I was especially fond of you and I always thought that of the three of you, you would be the one to never turn your back on me. Boy was I wrong! I was truly blindsided by your disappearance. The day you told me that you weren't ready to have a relationship with the family—I cried from Belleville to Orange. I was crushed! I do realize that a lot of your apprehension is based on your disorder, but I miss you terribly. I wonder how you are, if you have children, where you are, are you happy, do you ever think about me or your sister and brother? I remember how proud I always was of you in your intelligence, your mildness, and your independence. I always knew you would be able to take care of yourself. I cry every Mother's Day, Xmas, New Year, and August 26th, every time I get a year older with missing you! I really hope I get to see you before I leave this earth.

Savoring Eden

To my eldest son: You are a dear heart. You perhaps are more like me than anyone. Forgive me for passing that onto you. You are easily hurt. Although you say that you are here to help me, it hasn't truly been the case. I am more in debt than I have ever been, my household has been disrupted, my furniture has been ruined, and I am back into an emotional state I had hoped never to revisit. This is not to say that I do not appreciate your intent or your desire to be there for me. I love you for all of that and much more.

You do, however, harbor some anger towards me. It rears its head every so often by your tone of voice and the fact that you rarely do the things I ask you to do that would make cohabitating more bearable—like cleaning the living room and dining room or straightening up the back room to make it a bedroom or your office. You have to be aware that I am unhappy—that I cannot invite any of my friends here—that all of my hard work at decorating has been undone. You've hidden bills, not paid bills on time, and not repaid me for monies I had set aside for my publication fees, not to mention that my credit has been ruined in the process.

I know that you are depressed. I know that you miss your children. I know that you think that you are doing the best that you can. Please forgive me for being your enabler. I should have demanded more of you. I should have handled my own affairs. I should have just charged you rent and paid my own bills so that they would have stayed connected. I should have done a lot of things—but I didn't! So, it's my fault!

I do know that you love me. I am so proud that you feel that I did my best for you in your childhood, that I introduced you to music and the arts, good food, etc. I am glad that your memories are more of fun than misery. I wish that I could have been the parent you deserved. I wish you success and happiness in all of your endeavors. Please forgive me for all of my indiscretions and mistakes that may have caused you harm.

Patricia Ann Woolfork

To PJ, Jalen, and Kristen: I have loved you since the day you were born. I hope that you have good memories of me and that you enjoyed the time we have spent with each other. I miss you and I think of you daily. Remember our days at the pool and all of the good food I made for you. Oh, and don't forget Sonic's and McDonald's! PJ don't forget our wrestling matches.

To Kayla, John, and India: I love you very much. I am sorry that we aren't closer. I really miss having the opportunity to spend fun time with you— like going to the beach or to the movies or out to eat on a regular basis. I wish I had been able to buy you more toys and clothes. I just wish I had been given the opportunity of really being your grandmother. I wish I had more pictures of you when you were little. However, I am proud of your accomplishments in school and of your talents. John, I love your cartoons. India, I like your style. Kayla, you are a beauty! I really loved your poem. Keep writing. You have talent. I hope you will remember the fun we had playing UNO and going to movie day at my church.

To my grandson, Russell: I hope the best for you. You have great athletic ability. I hope that you find a way to utilize it while you are in your prime. I want that you should get a degree in a field that you will be successful in and that you make your education your priority. I also hope that you find it in your heart to forgive your Dad for all the things you think he did wrong, or for all the things he did not buy you and that you remember how much he loves you and has always loved you; that you remember that he did want you to live with him and that he did reach out to you, but your girlfriend was more important to you.

It is my hope that you have fond memories of me and the time we did spend with each other. You will always have a special place in my heart because you are my firstborn grandchild. You are a handsome young man. You have great potential. Handle your anger, life is too short. It will only cripple you and keep you unable to focus on what really matters in this life. Be forgiving—it is healing to the mind, soul and spirit. Reach out to your father. He misses you, and he, too, is hurting. Be an example to your brothers and sisters and your little cousins. We are all proud of you and want the very best that life has to offer you. Grab it and don't let it go!

To my son-in-law: I have loved you almost as long as my daughter first loved you. You are like a son to me, not a son-in-law. It's come to my attention that I have been accused of an indiscretion with regard to your mother. If this is so, please believe me that I have no recollection of having committed such an error. And, if I did, in fact, say anything about her illness—it was not malicious. It would have been to say that she had suffered enough and was now at peace together with her granddaughter. I certainly would never say or do anything to hurt you—I'd rather cut off a limb than to cause you any pain. I know how much you loved your mother. I only wish that your sister had called me. She had my number if she really thought I had done something like that. Or if even you had called me—but I had to get it third hand, unable to even defend myself.

I was a little hurt that you did not respond to my Father's Day greeting. I guess maybe this incident occurred around that time. I don't know when or who told this version to you. I only hope that you will find it in your heart to forgive me, if you believe that I did this. I am also sorry that you and the children are in the middle of the mess with my child and me. I know that you must maintain your loyalty to keep your own sanity. Hopefully we can resume our familial relationship with forgiveness and grace all around.

I have done everything I could to be there for you and your entire family. It pains me that I cannot talk to you or the kids, or that I am no longer welcome in your home. At least that is the understanding I have. If I am wrong about that, I would certainly like to be informed if it isn't already too late by the time you read this. At any rate, please accept my apologies for my many errors real or imagined—I have always had the best of intentions. I never meant to hurt anyone.

Now all of that aside, I just wanted to take this opportunity to express what has been on my mind of late. I am about to go under surgery in about ten days. Although it is supposedly a non-life-threatening procedure, unusual things can happen. I wish I were feeling more confident than I am. I am depending on God to bring me through this with flying colors. I only wish that I knew that my family was pulling for me and that they loved me.

I have been fighting the feeling that I have never been appreciated for who and what I am. I fear that I have gone through life without ever having unconditional love from anyone. All of my loves has come with a price attached. Everything was expected of me, and I was not to expect anything in return. I feel all used up.

I had children so that I would never have to be lonely, and yet I have been alienated from two of my children. If it's because of my actions, I take responsibility. However, I did the best I could with the limited resources and role models set before me. I've tried to be caring and loving despite my lack of it growing up. I still long for it so much so that I've allowed myself to be walked on, dismissed, disrespected, misjudged, ad nauseam.

I don't know how much time I have left on this earth. I do know that I have wasted enough of it searching for a nearly unattainable goal—happiness. I can't get it from other people. I must find it within myself. I only hope that it's not too late.

If I must continue my journey alone, I won't really be alone, because God—The Father, Son, and Holy Spirit will never leave me or desert me no matter what mistakes I make along the way. They know my heart and all of my motives. God knew what He was getting when He made me! He loves me anyway.

I hope that you all find your peace and your purpose. I hope that my life has some significance in yours. Whether you like it or not, my DNA is coursing either through your veins or your children's. I will never really ever disappear.

When you least expect it, you will say something you heard me say—that you vowed you would never say. You will look in the mirror and see an expression on your face that you once saw on mine. When you least expect it, you will do something I did—that you swore to God you would never do—almost the exact same way that I did it!

And when I am finally gone . . . you will remember that you really did love me in spite of everything! I wish I could have been there to hear it and see it and feel it.

With heartfelt sincerity, I remain,
Patricia Ann Woolfork   July 10, 2009

Update: My relationship with my daughter has become much more loving, understanding, and supporting. I still have not spoken to my middle child, 23 years and counting. My eldest son has given me two new granddaughters, and he is still being creative in his art, music, and writing. I have four grands in college and three in high school. My eldest grandson is married and has given me my first grand—a granddaughter. I am blessed. Tracey – you know how much I love you! (2018)

Sometimes It Sucks to be Me

Let Me Count the Ways

1. Being an only child puts too much responsibility on one person when your mother gets dementia and she tells you that your best isn't good enough. Nothing new to hear from her, but now you have to believe she doesn't know what she is saying after a lifetime of verbal, physical, and emotional abuse.
2. I have to always be the strong one. When my best friend, LaVonne passed, there was no one I could really show my real feelings of loss to because they were counting on me to hold it all together. I had to hide most of my tears, hold back on hugging for fear of falling apart, and stay busy to the point of exhaustion to prevent a primal scream from escaping from my mouth as it did on the evening I learned of her passing. The hardest thing I have ever had to do was eulogize my sister/friend and look at her body for the first time. I received only one sympathy card, and my church wouldn't even put my loss in its bulletin because I wasn't immediate family even though we were related by marriage and 57 years of best sister/friendship.
3. I am always in pain because of fibromyalgia or some other form of getting older and fatter malady.
4. I feel underappreciated and always an afterthought or when it is convenient for my family.
5. I am always the one to do the calling, offer the help, and the one to try to start and maintain a new acquaintance.
6. My brain never shuts down. I am always processing something. I don't sleep like I should.
7. I am lonely and lonesome at the same time.
8. Life seems to be getting harder instead of easier as I get older.
9. I put on a good face, but I have been sad most of my life and I get tired of it sometimes.

10. I feel abandoned and unloved now that LaVonne is gone, and I don't know how to process it. This pain is too great. My tears drip down my face on a daily basis.

But I did say "Sometimes" right?

I do have times when I feel great, I look pretty, I feel happy and blessed, and I have a really awesome day. There are days when I don't worry about how to pay Verizon, or how I will put food in my refrigerator. There are times that I truly believe that God will supply all of my needs, give me beauty for ashes, and He will restore my soul.

I am grateful for my sanity and the gift of writing that God gave me to work through being molested by my father, raped by a cousin, beaten and verbally abused by my husband, and cheated on with another man. Let's not forget the bloody welts left by my mother's black strap or being tied to a chair, gagged and blindfolded and put into a dark closet for hours—or being made to eat food out of the garbage because I wasn't supposed to waste food. Oh and how about being told I was never wanted, that I was just a responsibility, or that I would never amount to anything and that I was dumb, stupid, and ugly?

Sometimes, I am very productive and able to impart inspiration for others by using my words. Sometimes, my words can make others see the beauty in nature, the wisdom that comes with experience, bring comfort in times of loss, stir passions, provoke thought, and offer a sense of oneness in this journey called life with its many peaks and valleys.

I really think I am more positive than negative. I still believe in the innate goodness in people. I always strive to be and do my best. I try to be encouraging and offer guidance to both my children and grandchildren.

I refuse to let my past control my today and tomorrow. I was created for a purpose. I was made stronger by my trials and tribulations. I thrive not just survive!

Patricia Ann Woolfork

I am learning each day to love myself more. I am learning to stay true to myself and not change those parts of myself that are sincere, caring, out-going, friendly, helpful, intelligent and loving just to be accepted by others that are not capable of reciprocity. Their loss!

I did say, "Sometimes It Sucks to be Me," but not today!

COLOR ME

Color me Red . . .
>My heart is full of love of self and humanity.

Color me Blue . . .
>I am most beautiful when
>>I show compassion and empathy.

Color me Green . . .
>I am both alive and creative.

Color me Black . . .
>I am saddened by
>>Man's inhumanity.

Color me Yellow . . .
>I am full of bright ideas.

Color me Brown . . .
>I am secure, warm, and comforted.

Color me White . . .
>Because with the absence of color,
>>There is no bigotry or hatred.

Color me Orange . . .
>I am aglow with
>>Hope for a brighter tomorrow!

Color me . . .
>Pastel, Diffused, Muted, Vibrant,
>>Saturated, Neon, Intense, Primary,
>>>Secondary, and Tertiary
>>>>– Every shade and hue –

I want to become a Reflection of You!

Dear Patricia,

Why have you been so hard on yourself? Why can't you see what others see in you? Why are you afraid to succeed? Why are you so afraid of being alone? Why do you need to not take risks? Why can't you be happy?

I know life has dealt you a bad hand. So what! You are not the only one. The question is: What are you going to do now? You've learned a lot of new coping skills. You know now that you were co-dependent. Are there behavioral modifications you can now incorporate in your daily living?

Can you say, "No," when necessary? Can you stop being everyone else's caretaker and take care of yourself for a change? You know what you want. You wrote a beautiful poem about it. Can you make some of these desires come true even if there's no one to share it with? How about doing it for yourself? Aren't you worth it?

What about your goal to get published? Are you really actively pursuing that goal? Or, are you procrastinating as usual?

What about your housing problem? Have you decided what steps you will take to solve it? Why are you afraid of change? Could moving actually be a good thing? Do you want to still be an emotional whore, led around by somebody else's immature thinking and manipulation?

Don't you think you've survived enough heartache and trauma to satisfy many lifetimes? I believe that you have. I know you have the courage and strength, the know-how, and drive to aim for the best, and get it.

You say you want your life to make a difference for others. Make your life count for yourself as well. You have many talents. Maybe they weren't inherited, but rather developed in you by teachers and encouraged by peers. They are talents nonetheless. Are you going to throw that faith in you displayed by others back into their faces? Were their opinions invalid, inconsequential, or unimportant? Hardly!

You believed in yourself before. Do it again. Take inventory of your accomplishments:

1. You survived childhood sexual, physical, and mental abuse.
2. You graduated from high school #63 in a class of 463 students.
3. You kept what was left of your virtue until marriage.
4. You survived an abusive marriage.
5. You were a good role model for your children for educational pursuits, cultural enrichment, tenacity, keeping them fed, clothed, and sheltered.
6. You loved your family to the best of your ability, single handedly.
7. You went to college at age 27 with three small children and still managed to be on the Dean's List each semester. You graduated with a 3.81GPA. You were inducted into five Honor Societies. You graduated Magna cum laude with a BA Degree in English: Speech/Theatre/Media and Secondary English Education.
8. You taught and inspired your students and helped them mold their futures.
9. You write beautiful heartfelt poetry and prose that stir the emotions of others less verbal or gifted in writing as well as other writers who find your words inspiring and moving.
10. Your children have reached adulthood with minimal problems. They are confident, resourceful, highly intelligent, talented, and have had good home training.
11. You are a loving grandmother.
12. Your grandson adores you.
13. You've had the courage to face your demons head on.
14. You are a kind, considerate, intelligent, thoughtful person.
15. You have kept your sensitivity despite adversity.
16. You have positively impacted, encouraged, and motivated others by sharing yourself, your knowledge, and your experiences with them.

Relish these accomplishments. You have done well. Most of all, you have survived. You are a warrior. Your best is yet to come, and you are on the right track. Remember to take care of yourself first. Remember that you are worth it.*

Sincerely,

That inner voice that is you, Patricia Ann

1994 Radar Institute, Illinois—assignment to write letter of encouragement to self

MAYBE TOMORROW

Telephone line quiet.
Doorbell silent.
Music in the background mellow.
Mood low
Expectations high.
Disappointment – great.

There is no phone call.
No one at the door.
Music the only comfort.
Words of love sung by strangers
Sustains the hope –
Maybe tomorrow.

OPEN LETTER TO SELF

Dear_____:

Today is the beginning of the rest of your life. I want for you all that you have ever desired, yearned for, contemplated, dreamed about to become part of your reality.

I know that buried somewhere deep in your innermost resources, you possess the ability to do and achieve wondrous things if only you begin to see what others already see in you. You are talented, poised, attractive, and kind in spirit and nature. You deserve both happiness and success; and you will get them both if you only begin to believe in yourself and your potential.

Remember that nothing truly worth having is easily attained. With success comes preparation, hard work, and, at times, disappointment. Just remain focused on the fact that hardship and disappointment are but momentary phases which one must encounter along the way. You can be loved by many and you can share your love with many, if first you love yourself. There is no one or anything more worthy of love than you are right now.

There is nothing to be done about yesterday because it has already passed. Let yesterday be as a fallen leaf blown away by a gust of wind—a snowflake on warmed earth. Learn to forgive those who have hurt you, be it intentional or otherwise; and most of all, learn to forgive yourself!

You are worthy. You are worthy of love; you are worthy of success; you are worthy of happiness; and you are worthy of every dream you've ever dreamed coming true be it for yourself or your family.

Remember that most of our hurt is caused by good intent gone awry—not from pure malice. The negativity you have filtered through your life's blood was caused by ignorance and/or indifference. It was not because of wrong-doing on your part.

Accept the person that you are right now, not out of resignation, because who you are is valid even if you don't think you are the best you can be. Your best is just around the corner.

Believe in yourself as others already believe in you. Believe that your essence is important and that you impact on others each and every day without even realizing it. You have the power within to change not only your life but the lives of others as well.

Now is the beginning of the rest of your life. Now you will learn what makes you tick, what makes you react, and what brings you either pain or joy. Now is your time to soul search without inhibition, without shame, without hesitation.

During this Journey, expose your vulnerability, your fears, your phobias, your insecurities. Face them head on with pride and determination and the assurance that you may come out scathed, but without mortal wounds. Lick those scratches if you must; but remember, as with any scar, first comes the scab and then the healing!

With belief and faith in yourself, you have the power to become healthy, wealthy, and wise. Your Journey has only begun. Buckle up and enjoy the ride!*

Loving you always,

1990, Delmar, California

POSTSCRIPT

The real fear is that I won't like the new me any better than the old me! I guess only time will tell, huh?

You know, last night looking at the waves, I had a momentary desire to become one with the sea? Crossing the highway, I wanted to become a part of anyone's fender. But, alas, I really could be close to finding the answer to "Who am I?" It would be a pity to get this close and not succeed.

Is a miracle too much to ask for after all? Why am I feeling so God awful alone? Why can't I try to break out of this frame of mind and enjoy the beauty around me without feeling out of place and out of touch? Why can't I enjoy a walk on the beach without mourning for a companion with whom to share the experience and in so doing minimize my own joy of watching the waves ebb and flow.

Help me, please, to get over me! You are one of the most spectacular people I know, and I love you very much. You have yourself to be friends with. Start liking yourself!*

1990, Delmar, California

WHAT IT MEANS TO BE LONELY

Lonely is waking in the middle of the night
Only to find an empty pillow
On the other side of the bed.
Lonely is having a call-wait telephone
That never rings.
Lonely is waiting for the lover that never shows.
Lonely is having no one with which to share
The events of the day.
Lonely is having no one to call your own –
Someone who shares
Your joy and disappointments,
Happiness and sorrow.
Lonely is Christmas morning
Without a single present under the tree.
Lonely is singing "Auld Lang Syne" to yourself.
Lonely is having no one say
That you have been missed.
Lonely is having no one say, "I love you."
Lonely is . . .
Looking into the mirror and seeing . . .
Nothing.

MEDITATION

I lay here thinking
Of all the things I am feeling –
Groping for the words to explain
The things that affect my soul, my spirit,
My very being –
The turbulence within me.

What am I feeling at this point and time in my life?
I think that it is love.
But what is love?
Is it needing someone or
Wanting to be with one person only?
Is it enjoying every spare moment with one individual?
Is love wanting to find protection and comfort
In the strong arms of a warm, loving man?
Is love identifying with music and beautiful poetry?

Why are my feelings rushing around
So tumultuously within my small frame?
Why can't I feel free
To express my innermost thoughts?
Why do I feel guilty for wanting
A part of life that I have every right to share in?
Why do I need love so badly?

Who am I really?
The modest, moral, upstanding person I strive to be?
Who am I?
A woman who is warm, loving, young and vital –
Who wishes to love and care,
Yes, pamper, spoil, and cherish
Someone who wants to belong only to me?

Savoring Eden

Who am I?
A person in love
With being loved, appreciated and needed.
Someone who dreams and must continue to dream
For fear that when awake –
Nothing in life is as beautiful.

What am I?
I am not a liberated soul
I find life disappointing.
I am unfulfilled.
I am alone.
I am confused.

I wonder what my values really are
And why I expect so much from life
And why none of my expectations are met.

I am in a vacuum –
If only someone would release me
Like the proverbial genie.
However, to be released
Could mean my destruction
So,
Here I remain.

TEMPEST

How can I share love, give love, show love
When I've never been taught?
How do I become happy
When all I've ever experienced has been sorrow?
How do I laugh
When tears are rushing against my eyes like
The tide crashing against the shore?

Despair and forlorn encompass me as though
They were tidal waves.
I search,
I run,
I look for a secure place in which to hide myself
Until this storm of unhappiness passes over.

Inside me there is an overwhelming,
Overpowering loneliness.
To feel wanted, needed, and appreciated
To be happy instead of sad,
To be whole instead of just half of a person,
To be the most, the best I can be.
To be free in all possible ways,
To remain sensitive, yet strong,
To be at peace with myself and those around me.
Is all in life I ever hope to achieve.

Unhappiness has a strangle-hold on me –
Killing me!
I must fight.
I need to break free!

I am at the edge,
The brink of insanity.
One more push –Just a little nudge – I'm there!
In the still of the night I cry out,
"Help me"!

Savoring Eden

"Please"?
No reassuring word.
No one to say, "I love you."

Fear engulfs me.
My body is tense.
I want to SCREAM!
Perhaps that will release this pressure.

I want to cry like an infant,
But there is no one to comfort me.
My faith is shaky –
Perhaps there is none.

I am helpless.
I can't keep us with this endless turmoil.
It's overtaking me.
"Help," I cry!
Love me!
Please?
Someone?

Let me find a little joy.
Let me find a little calm.
Let me find a rainbow
When this storm of discontent is over.
Let me find love, or at best,
Let me become satisfied with my life.

If none of this be feasible,
Let me cease to live.
Let me sleep,
At least then I will find eternal peace.

Patricia Ann Woolfork

DEAR MOMMIE, JUNE 1, 1994

Today I am writing this letter to ask you about something that has always been on my mind. Why don't you love me? Is there some awful deed I've done that I've buried in my subconscious?

Do you remember telling me that you didn't want me, never loved me, that I was only a responsibility? Did you really mean those things or were you simply pushing me away to get away from you own pain, unhappiness, and suffering?

Did someone molest or abuse you as a child? Is that why you beat me, blindfolded, gagged, and tied me to a chair and put me in a dark closet when I was little? Or, did you really see me as the "bad seed" like in the movie?

Why didn't you protect me from Daddy? Why didn't you sleep with him when he wanted you to? Why didn't you believe me when I told you he molested me? Why did you send me away instead of him? Why did I have to live in the projects with nasty Aunt Julia and the roaches and stinking elevators? Why didn't you take me away without me having to lie and say it never happened?

Have I ever done anything to make you proud of me, to love me? Why do you have more compassion and love for strangers you try to preach to than you have for me?

Why did you beat me until I had welts or cuts on my body? Why did you pinch me so deeply that pieces of meat came off of me?

I know you know what it's like to be unhappy. I've experienced the rage your own unhappiness has caused you. Why do the words "I love you" choke in your throat? Why have you abandoned me? All of my life all I wanted from you was to be loved and accepted for who and what I am, unconditionally. I love you unconditionally!

I hold no grudges, no animosity toward you for the physical and mental abuse you vented upon me. I love you. I miss you. I need you. My inner child was betrayed by Daddy and abandoned by Mommie. I've always felt unloved and unlovable.

I thought you would have forgiven me when I got baptized, but you didn't. You told me that I had ruined your life. Don't you know, deep in your heart, that I was a child, and it was Daddy's fault? Won't you take some responsibility for what happened to me when I was eleven? Won't you help me get over this shame and guilt so that I can heal?

I am taking the appropriate steps to get better mentally, physically, emotionally, and spiritually. I want to do it with you. My health is not good. I wrote to you last summer telling you about my heart attack, but you never answered me. You have a telephone that I cannot call, and you won't call me collect. Now I hear that you are divorcing your husband (long overdue). Are you divorcing me, also?

Please allow me the courtesy of an answer to all of these long overdue questions. Please tell me what is in your heart. I know you are not the sentimental type, and I am all the more sorry for you for all the emotions you have kept buried your entire life.

I hope that you are questing for inner peace and tranquility. Please be assured that I would love to share that space with you as mother and daughter. I've already lost my childhood, and it cannot be restored, but our future together is still in the making.

We are both growing older, hopefully wiser. Can't we both stop acting juvenile and forgive, forget, and love one another for the time we have left so neither of us will have any regrets—knowing we've done all that we can. Our last visit together was the best ever. You said that yourself. Did you mean it? There's a great-grandson that should know the love of his great-grandmother. I'd love for you to see him again and experience his eagerness to learn and explore, to feel his innocence, and the sweetness of his kisses on your cheeks. Oh, what you are missing! He has brought me so much joy. Every time he sees your picture on my dresser he says, "Nannu's Mommie."

Well, aside from saying "I'm sorry" for the last time, I can only say if you want or need a daughter, I still have first dibs on the job (smile.) If my application is no longer acceptable, please be woman enough to let me know, in writing, so that I can get on with my life—either embrace you or mourn your loss. That's only fair. It's up to you now.*

As always, I love you,

Patricia Ann

This is my confrontation letter to my mother written while at Radar Institute in Illinois in 1994 and mailed registered mail.

TO MY MOTHER, BETTYE M. WOOLFORK

I know you did your best.
I forgive your mistakes.
You made me stronger because of them.
I turned out okay.
My God already had a plan for me.
Thank you for all that you did do right.

I have fashion sense,
Social grace,
Culinary excellence,
And so much more.

Without you and the childhood I lived through,
I would never have become the writer/poet I am today.
This is my legacy.

Although it was Dementia
That finally gave me the mother
I always yearned for,
I am grateful and pleased to be your daughter,
Receive the hugs and kisses I never got, and
Be re-introduced ad infinitum as "your only baby."
It warms my healing heart.

I LOVE YOU, and
I am blessed
To have you with me at 86 years of age
Dementia and all.

12/29/15

Patricia Ann Woolfork

FATHER'S DAY, JUNE 19, 1994

Father,

I wish that I could write some sentimental words to tell you how great a father you have been, but who are we kidding?

I do want to take this opportunity to thank you for working to help keep a roof over my head, clothes on my back, and food in my mouth. And, however unfortunate it is, this is all that I can thank you for. I told you over the phone that I would be writing this letter. Well, that time has now arrived.

I wish I could be devoid of all feeling for you, but you are my father, and some feelings cannot be erased, only modified. I loved you once. There was a five-year little girl that adored her daddy so much that she wanted to marry him when she got grown up. That little girl no longer exists.

There were many times in my childhood when you came to my aid when I was sat the hands of my mother. I can say "thank you" for those times. But, where were you when she blindfolded me, gagged me, tied me to a chair and put me into the closet? Why didn't you stop her from beating skin off of my body, making me bleed in the process? Where were you when she was telling me that I was stupid and ugly—I looked just like you? Where were you when she told me she loved my brother, and her pregnancy with me caused his death? Where were you when she told me that she never loved me or wanted me, and that I was only a responsibility?

Why didn't you rescue me from the mental and physical abuse she dished out on me? Why did you let her blame me for a miscarriage when we lived on Seymour Avenue? Why did you allow her to beat me over a disconnected telephone on Peshine Avenue? Why didn't you stop her from making me eat out of the trash after food had been in dishwater and thrown away? Why did you allow her to pinch plugs of meat out of me? You were both guilty of child abuse—you for allowing it—she for committing its action.

I always thought that you had no balls when it came to Mommie. So you chose to drink yourself to death on weekends. What a fine example you showed me as you puked all over the bathroom floor or on your bed. A stench returns to my nostrils now as I write about it all these years later.

My knight's shining armor was rusted. And now, I address your crimes against me: I remember you bathing me and rubbing me hard between my legs. Was it a preamble to your later sexual overtures? I thought . . . I must really be dirty there! I thought nothing of Daddy washing a little girl of seven or eight. Could you tell me if it was you or Mommie that used the comet on the washrag?

At age eleven . . . why did you turn to me for sex? Did I seduce you? Did I want to put on Mommie's nightgown? Why did you make me lie about the blood on the bedspread? Why did you make me see the next weekend come?

I still smell your breath and feel your thick slobbering tongue kisses. I still see images of you trying to enter my tiny body, and you having me lay on top of you as you masturbated between my thighs. You told me how much you loved me and how unhappy you were with Mommie, and I still adored you then. I did not know it was wrong to feel pity for someone you loved. Yet, when I wanted it to stop and told on you, I became "a liar and a slut."

I had to leave my home, my room, my toys, and live in the projects with your nasty sister. Did you know that my cousins Melvin and Gwendolyn both molested me when I was there? Do you know that is why I lied to come back home? I know now that you touched Melvin. He became a pedophile just like you and molested his own daughter(s), too.

You took my virginity and innocence from me. You alienated my mother from me—not a difficult task in the first place! You betrayed my trust. You lost my respect. I loved you, and I hated you. I still do. You never once told me that you were sorry. You never once took responsibility as the adult in the situation. You never owned up to your incest with your own daughter!

How has this affected me? I became an emotional orphan. I had neither a father or a mother to love me. I began to feel worthless and unlovable. I felt dirty—used goods. I was afraid someone else would find out and hate me.

I lost my friend Didi after you dragged me around the corner with a gun, going after her brother, Louie, the night I told the police on you. Did you have anything to do with her sister's death? She was found strangled in an abandoned building not long after I turned you in. I often wondered about that, but I was too scared to know.

How has my growing up with you affected me? I watched you beat my mother, punch her in her face, slap her. I watched and listened to you crawl around my bedroom floor asking her to come sleep with you. I saw stars when you slapped me in my eye when I questioned you. I remember trying to stab you with a fork to make you stop hurting my mother.

How has my childhood affected my life? What childhood? I never had one. I look at my pictures and I see sad eyes even when I am smiling. I see a depressed teenager devoid of friends outside of school—no social life.

What about when I was married to Henry? You heard him beating me upstairs, but you never intervened. Why? Was it okay because you used to do it? What about when your nephew, Sam, raped me? Did you go after him, or was that okay, too?

Every heartache, every bad relationship, I blame you. You taught me that all I was good for was a quick "fuck." I wasn't shown how to love properly. I kept looking for the daddy I lost in other men. I wanted to hear you say, "I'm sorry," and confess to my mother. I am afraid to get close. I sometimes have flashbacks of you when I am making love and have a panic attack. I've been unhappy all of my life, and I blame you for that! I blame Mommie for that, too.

I did not ask to come here. If I wasn't wanted, you should have given me away. I feel so terribly lonely. You've never even tried to make amends after I became an adult.

Now I have to ask myself, "If you did it to me, did you also molest my daughter." She's displayed all the classic symptoms. If you did not go all the way, did you touch her inappropriately? I really need to know so that I can help her. I don't want her condemned to a lifetime of hell and misery.

I don't give a damn about our relationship. You rarely communicate with me anyway. You let my Aunt Mattie get buried without so much a call or a drive-by to let me know she was dead. You don't let me know when you are going to see my mother so that I can go along. You don't let me know about family reunions. You treat your other kids better than me or mine. You run to New York but can't come the five miles to see me.

You used me to be unfaithful to Rose. You bring me two little girls and expect me to accept them as sisters. Are they your future victims of love? Check yourself. Don't let history repeat itself. It is never too late to get some help. You told me you never thought you did anything wrong. Well, think again!

You have a 45-year-old daughter who has lost most of her youth to depression, suicidal thoughts, feelings of self-hatred, guilt, and fear of abandonment.

Do I blame you? Hell, yes! Do I forgive you? Sometimes, yes—other times, no. I want to. Perhaps. The terms must be mine.

Until you sit down with me, face-to-face, and confront this issue—I have nothing else to say to you. I'll give you the same choice I gave to your soon to be ex-wife, my mother: I want to either embrace you as my father or mourn your loss. I must put all of this shit behind me. I'd like to do it with you. If not, so be it!

Patricia Ann Woolfork

You know my phone number, but in case it's been misplaced, it is _____. Use it or lose it. It is up to you, but don't wait too long to decide.

This was my confrontation letter written while at Radar Institute in Illinois. It was mailed to my father by registered mail. He eventually asked my forgiveness before he died in 1998.

Dear Daddy,

I thought about you today, and it brought tears to my eyes. It occurred to me that I haven't finished grieving for you. Will I ever be done?

Today I thought about the times we played cards until you found it necessary to cheat (smile). I miss having someplace to go when I needed to feel grounded. I miss our spats. I miss seeing your face.

I had to be honest with myself today. I have been so busy trying to act like my losing you was no big deal, that I lost touch with my feelings about you. I still harbor the fact that I didn't respect you as a man, as a person, but I never stopped loving you as my Daddy.

Sometimes I am still angry about what you did to disrupt my childhood and the pain you caused me with my child, but I have forgiven you in my innermost heart. I know now that you were mentally ill and perhaps with your upbringing, you really didn't know any better! It still was no excuse for abusing my child or the other little girls you ruined. My eldest child resents that he didn't get to have the mother that God originally created me to become because I was damaged by both you and Mommy. I often wonder, what if . . . ?

Here I am about to turn 50 years old, and I am still that little girl looking for the love she didn't get! I am haunted by the fact that the first man to ever enter into my life betrayed me so completely, robbed me of my innocence, gave me a false sense of my worth as a female, and taught me how to love inappropriately.

Nevertheless, I have come to realize that in every relationship since, I have patterned my lovers after you. There have had two men in my life that were alcoholics, substance abusers, and batterers! I haven't a clue how to break the chain. I guess it starts with me taking better care of myself, loving me for who and what I am and what I have yet to become.

I am not that "slut" that you told Mommy I was that night that I told on you. I was not yours to fondle, probe, slobber upon, or penetrate! All these many years later, I can still smell the alcohol on your breath, tainted by the cigarette smoke on your teeth. I flash back at the most inopportune times. How do I explain this to my husband?

I am still hurting from the fact that very few people were there to even comfort me when you died. They claimed it was because of what you had done to both me and mine. BUT MY FATHER DIED! Where was the compassion for me and what I lost? Good, bad, indifferent, I lost a part of myself when you were put in that casket.

I loved you so much when I was a little girl. All little girls love their daddies. All little girls want to marry daddy until they learn differently. Yet, I was deprived of even that childhood fantasy because of an insecure mother and a perverted father. I loved you even when you didn't protect me from the beatings, the tie downs in the closet, the scalding baths, and the rage that was the result of your misbehavior as an adult.

But now the question surfaces and battles against the insides of my brain . . . how long did the abuse really last? My memories are coming back to me like flashes in a pan. I remember the baths and the hard scrubbing and rubbing you did between my legs. That was happening long before I was eleven. I look at my photographs when I was four or five years old and my eyes are haunted and sad. Did I ever have a happy moment as a child? Did I ever feel special?

I do remember thinking that I must have been adopted very early in my life. Maybe my intuition was telling me that something was horribly wrong. Maybe I always knew that my mother never wanted me. I know how often she told me how much she wanted my brother and that I was the cause of his death by being born first and causing her to have the blood transfusion. She has even said that had he lived, if she brought him home, I probably would have killed him! I was one years old. Go figure!

Oh, how vividly I remember the closet and the blindfold and gag, the ropes and the hours in the dark. I suppose that is why I freaked out the first time my electricity was turned off. How I remember being called the "bad seed!" I've seen that movie since I became an adult. How could anyone think of their child in that manner? Oh, I also remember eating eggs out of the garbage because I had tried to cook and didn't like them. I still taste the coffee grinds and the dish soap that was in them. I remember how often I was told that I was an embarrassment simply doing childish things. I remember how other children were treated better than me when they visited us. I remember the hateful remarks.

I remember being thrown out of the house when I told on you. I remember living in the filthy projects with your nasty sister and her eight kids. I remember being molested by her son while I was there. I remember wanting to come home because it was a horror I was already familiar with.

Oh, how I wanted to be a good girl so Mommy and Daddy would love me and be proud of me. Nothing I ever did was enough to not have you two fighting or to bring you home on the weekends without the cursing and the puking. I thought if I loved you enough, you would love me back.

My reality is . . . actions speak louder than words. You and my mother acted like you never wanted me or loved me unconditionally. The sad part of that reality is that you didn't really love yourselves or each other, so how could there be any for me? And thus, how do I learn to love myself? How do I know what love is? Would I be able to recognize love, if it bit me on my ass? Will I ever find it within or outside of myself? Am I love-able? Still, I hunger for the love my mother was incapable of giving and agonize over the love you offered.

I really want peace, Daddy. I thought I would have it when you died, but it still has not arrived. I know that it will come when I tell my story of abuse. Yet, something inside tells me that I am betraying you. I know that it is simply me avoiding a painful truth, exposing my not so perfect life as an only child. I am still protecting my perpetrators—still hiding the family secrets. When will I ever learn to stop caring about what other people will think of me?

Yes, I have done a many a stupid thing as a result of my upbringing. Many things I regret doing and some I would never repeat if given the chance. I did what I thought would get me the love I so desperately needed. I settled for less than I truly deserved because I was taught that I wasn't worth much and nothing of value was expected from me. What a treacherous thing to do to an innocent child placed in your care by God! How I trusted you and believed in you! How I felt your pain and tried to make it all better!

And now here I sit because today I cried for you. I shed many tears because I was not at the hospital when you died. I wept for the father I was deprived of. I cried because I haven't had a good cry. I cried because I left your ashes in the park and I haven't anywhere to go and talk to you. I cried because I miss you. I cried because I love you. I cried because I hate you for what you did to me and my child. I cried because I didn't get to say goodbye.

I cried because you didn't prepare me to make better choices in men. I cried because I wasn't allowed to cry freely when you died. I cried because I feel abandoned. I cried because my soul aches. I cried just because I don't know what else to do. I cried because I haven't had the "happy ever after".

I cried because "Daddy's little girl" doesn't have the same meaning that it had for other little girls. I cried because I don't think you knew any better. I cried because you didn't try to do better.

I cried because your blood flows through my veins, and I don't know how much of your sickness will contaminate my being. I cried because my heart is broken and it hasn't begun to heal.

I just thought you needed to know how I feel these days. I needed to be honest with myself about that! I trust that you are in a better place for I wish you no ill will. I have forgiven you. Now I need to forgive myself.

Your daughter,

Patricia Ann Woolfork
May 19, 1999

My father, Ulysses K. Woolfork, died on February 2, 1997. He did ask for my forgiveness for what he had done to me and my child before he died. I have recently learned other things about him that I will get around to writing about. It will not be pretty. I wish not to pass judgement, but I can probably guarantee that I will never shed another tear over that man, and he should be rotting in hell—cremation was just his preamble. (2018)

I AM A SURVIVOR!

I am a survivor.
I am your mother,
Your sister,
Your aunt,
Your cousin.

I am the elderly,
The middle-aged,
The young woman,
The girl.

I am a survivor.
I am an over-comer.
I am the one that would not surrender.

I am ever hopeful,
Always confident,
Full of grace,
Forever grateful for the victory.

I am a survivor.
Yet, others remain in my wake.
There are still battles to be fought and won.
Won't you join me in the fight?

DEAR LSJ, JUNE, 1994

I know that you are surprised to be getting this letter from me, but I hope you will continue to read its contents. I have come to a crossroad in my life. There are many things that have needed to be said over the years. I now have found the courage and the strength to say them. If you can locate that spot in your heart that used to love me, you will hear me out because this is the last time I will ever seek communication with you unless it pertains to our three beautiful, intelligent, creative, and resourceful children.

I didn't realize how much pain I had buried over these past twenty-one years, but because you were once so big a part of my life, I thought you should know how much you have affected my life. I had to delve deeply into my past over the last three weeks, and I was amazed at all the tiny detail that came popping into my mind.

I remember the first time I saw you at Clinton Place. I remember how thrilled I was to see you again at Weequahic High School. I remember our first kiss behind my locker door. I remember meeting you at the bus stop and walking to school holding hands. I remember our fights (especially over Marlene Sobel). I remember your singing "Fly Me to the Moon" to me.

I remember the first real poem I ever wrote was to you called, "Memories and Dream." I read it to my counselor the other day, and for the first time since I wrote it at age 15, I cried. Why did I cry? Let me count the reasons:
1. I cried for our innocence, our lost, our dreams, our lost expectations, and our children—that they were robbed of a family.
2. I cried for the memories. I remember writing my new last name hundreds of times.
3. I cried about our naming our children six years before they were even a reality or possibility.
4. I cried about not going to the prom with you because you were a different religion, and my mother would not allow it.
5. I cried about the fights I had with my mother over you.

Please hear me out! You were my life, my whole world! I remember how worried and scared I was for you all the while you were in Viet Nam. I remember the long letters, the declarations of love we shared. I remember my nightly prayers, every waking minute hoping that you would be brought back to me safely.

I remember shopping for my wedding suit. Do you remember it? It was a yellow and white daisy brocade coat and dress. I remember our getting the license, the blood test, and picking out the wedding bands.

I remember our almost making love the night before our wedding but stopping so that it could be a "holy wedding." I remember how handsome you looked. I remember our coming home with Mother and Teddy—they went to their room and we went to Margie's old room. I remember our being nervous and clumsy. I remember our laughing hysterically when we climaxed together for the first time. I was the princess who had found her Prince Charming. We would live happily ever after.

I remember the tearful good-byes when you had to leave to go to your last assignment in Colorado. I remember having to call you to let you know that Lance had died, and the tears we shared over the phone. And then I remember . . .

The letter you sent to me telling me that you had VD and that I should get checked. I remember you telling me you paid my doctor to falsify the blood test. I remember you telling me you got it from a prostitute in Nam. I remember that fearful trip to my gynecologist. I remember my sigh of relief when I tested negative. I remember forgiving you and coming to Colorado to start our life together. I remember our first little apartment. I remember our trying to make a baby. I remember our succeeding six months later. I remember our spats, our making up. I remember our buying our first house, 1129 East Moreno Avenue, Colorado Springs, Colorado. I remember buying our first car, a 1965 blue Ford Mustang. We were only 21 years old. I remember the birth of our son, our beautiful, beautiful Russell LaMont. We brought him from Fort

Carson's base hospital into his own house, into his own room. We had achieved the American Dream.

I remember your suicide attempt three months later. I remember you telling me that you were a homosexual after the base doctor told you that you must tell me. I remember asking if you were doing it since our marriage. I remember you telling me, "no." I remember forgiving you for your past, accepting you as my husband, telling you that I loved you. I remember you telling me how much you loved me, too.

I remember our first fight. We were driving back from Kmart because I had accidently scratched your face with my long nails, playing around. I thought you were playing, but you were serious. You had to sit on me to stop me from fighting back. You never did that again. I remember eventually making up.

I remember the birth of our second son, Vaughann Christian, my beautiful blue-eyed baby. I remember you holding my hand in delivery and being with me the whole time. You were on guard duty when our first child was born. I remember Mother, your mother, coming from New Jersey to meet her grandchildren, and to take care of me and the kids.

I remember the vacation we planned for nine months later so that both families could see the children. I remember having to leave you for two months so that you could save up the money for the airfare to meet us.

I remember telling you that I was pregnant again. I remember when, where, and how our baby was conceived – April 7, 1973. I remember almost losing our baby. I remember our love letters and phone calls. I remember missing you. And then . . .

I remember the letter I got from you two weeks before we were to join each other stating that you had slept with Sgt. Sapp, in our bed, and had committed a homosexual act with him. Why him of all people? He and his wife and children were our surrogate family, trusted friends. I trusted him!

I remember calling the Elders to confirm your story. I remember letting Mother read the letter, crying. I remember Mother telling me that I was the first and only girl you had ever paid attention to and loved and that if we loved each other, we could work it out. I remember Mother telling me how much she loved me and her grandchildren.

I remember feeling guilty for not being home with you. I remember taking the blame for your homosexuality. I could have, should have done something better, different. I remember the phone call telling you that I loved you and forgave you, but that I needed time to heal. I remember feeling betrayed.

I remember seeing at the airport and wanting to, but unable to, forget the pain. I remember telling you, again, that I loved you, but that I needed time. I remember the arguments over sex, your attempt to transfer your guilt onto me. I remember your verbal abuse—what you would do to me if you ever caught me cheating on you.

I remember leaving you a few weeks after we returned home because of the aforementioned arguments and threats. I didn't want a household of fighting like I had growing up. I remember the woman's shelter—one long room with single cots. Me, my son, Russell, age 2 and my son, Vaughann, age 11 months, and a three month old fetus, our future daughter, Heather-Michelle away from my family. I remember changing the name we had picked out because you had been so emotionally and verbally abusive that I didn't want you to know anything about the baby's birth or name.

I remember missing you, wanting you, being ripped apart by grief, not knowing how to compete, regretting letting you go, loving you, hating you—wanting to die—especially after I was told about your second suicide attempt.

I remember when you stopped paying the bills we had agreed upon and that the car was repossessed. The creditors wanted to take the furniture out of the house but opted for the car instead.

I remember going into labor at home alone. I remember LaVieta taking me to the hospital. I remember her being in the delivery room with me. I remember seeing our daughter being born, holding her as they cut the cord. I remember going into shock, hearing the nurses and three doctors working on me telling me to stay awake, stay with them. I could hear the codes being called over the loud speakers. I remember feeling at peace, singing a kingdom song as I lost consciousness. I was told that I had gone into shock twice and that they had almost lost me. The doctors told me that another child would kill me. I remember being angry because I had almost lost my life to prove your masculinity, not once but twice; I nearly died having our first child from hemorrhaging, and you are gone anyway!

I remember coming back to NJ. I remember Aunt Francis spotting me at K-Mart and telling you that I was back in Jersey. Forever etched in my memory is of when you came to see your children for the first time in two years—you wore a straw hat, a pair of clogs, a shoulder bag, and your lover, Joseph in tow. I felt betrayed yet again. Joseph was my friend in high school. I always knew he was gay. Were you dating him in school at the same time you were dating me? Did you bring him to my parent's house just to torment me further? I remember still loving you. I figured I would learn about sex and what men did to each other. I wanted you back—I had one more hole than Joseph. Do you remember Delaine's cocktail sip? We helped with the food, and then we made love. Do you remember getting out of bed with me and going home with Joseph? At the cocktail sip your sister was introducing me as your wife, and you walked in with Joseph. I sat the table and cried as I watched the two of you flaunting your gayness before me. I was so humiliated.

Do you remember telling me that keeping your kids "was not conducive to your lifestyle?" Well, you did. I would have them dressed and ready to spend time with you, and you wouldn't even call or show up. Then once I remarried, you wanted to be super-dad. Do you realize that Henry beat me every time I talked to you? Do you realize that once my marriage was ruined, you stopped being super-dad? It was almost as if you didn't want me, but you didn't want anyone else to have me.

Do you remember that we made love several times while you were married to Edith? You professed your love to me and that you wanted to come back because of the kids. Do you remember sleeping with me after your divorce and before your marriage to Sherrell? Do you remember asking me if you had done the right thing on your wedding day to her? You loving me and me loving you was so evident that even my mother saw it, and she told me, "let her have him?" She knew where my heart was, but I did not pursue.

Do you remember trying to take my children away from me because Sherrell could not have any? You tried to smudge my character to my children and to the judge when you tried to have me charged with fraud for working while on welfare.

Do you deny your past still? Have you told your wife the truth? Have you ever been honest with our children? I had always hoped that your relationship with your children would be different from the one you had with your dad. You often told me about the pain you experienced growing up. You've missed a lot of your own children's growth and development—I am sorry for you. I hope you do not have to wait until you are near death to have a relationship with them like you had to do with your father. Your sons have always needed to hear the truth from you—they have fears that only you can absolve. You ought to be honest with yourself. You have been living a lie for far too long—at my expense!

I have done lots of things that I am ashamed of. A lot of things were done to support my children. I blame you for that. I blame my present mental and emotional health on your lack of loyalty, compassion, understanding, trust, and lack of conscious. You have no reason to resent me or hate me unless it is because I remind you of your own guilt.

You were my whole world and now your children are my whole world—my grandson is my world. I am finally willing to let go. I have lost too much already. Mother is dead. Teddy is dead. Bernie is dead. Margie and Delaine no longer treat me as part of the family, and I thought that would always be, but that's your fault, too! I was there for your family when your parents died. I know now that favor won't be returned. You've turned your family against me? Why? I've known them since I was 15 years old.

When I read a poem that I wrote from my heart when Bernie died, you said, "She's quite the little actress, isn't she?" I had loved Bernie since he was three years old, and he died when he was 26. Where was your Christian kindness?

Well, at last I've come to the end of this dialogue. I hope you aren't too calloused and too self-righteous to be touched with remorse for the pain I have suffered because of your past indiscretions and lies.

I no longer wish to waste your time or mine with regret. The past cannot be changed, the present is manageable, and the future isn't promised. Continue to look out for yourself. You're really good at that!*

Patricia Ann
1994, Radar Institute, Illinois
Confrontation letter sent by registered mail

YOU HATE ME, WHY?

I reached out to you several times after your wife died to offer my sincere condolences for your loss, not just because you are the father of my children, but because I have known you since we were in seventh grade, and you were the first boy I ever loved and continued to love you. Besides, it is a Christian thing to do!

I got a distressing call from our daughter stating that you told her that you hate me; she was too upset to go into further details. You hate me, why? Hate is such an ugly word...

The Oxford Dictionary defines hate as a verb to mean to feel intense or passionate dislike for (someone). Its synonyms: loathe, detest, despise, dislike, abhor, and execrate. As a noun, its definition is intense or passionate dislike, "feelings of hate and revenge." Its synonyms: hatred, loathing, detestation, dislike, distaste, abhorrence, abomination, execration, aversion. The word hate is also used politely to express one's regret or embarrassment at doing something: "I hate to bother you." (1)

Merriam Webster Dictionary: (a) intense hostility and aversion usually deriving from fear, anger, or sense of injury. (b) extreme dislike or antipathy. (2)

In psychoanalysis, Sigmund Freud defined hate as an ego state that wishes to destroy the source of its unhappiness. More recently, The Penguin Dictionary of Psychology defines hate as a "deep, enduring, intense emotion expressing animosity, anger, and hostility towards a person, group, or object." Because hatred is believed to be long-lasting, many psychologists consider it to be more of an attitude or disposition than a temporary emotional state. (3) (4)

Macmillan Dictionary: verb (transitive) to dislike someone or something very much. (a) If you hate something such as a particular situation or activity, you find it unpleasant or upsetting. (b) used for saying that a particular situation or event would make you feel unhappy, (c) as a metaphor: hate, jealousy, and other negative feelings are like poisons or diseases, or like something that is destroying you from inside. (5)

Now that all of the defining has been done, and by definition all bases have been covered, let us address why you could possibly hate me after so many years and time has passed between us.

- Could the main reason be that I left our marriage after you slept in our bed with an army buddy of yours?
- Could you hate me because I stayed with you after you confessed to being bi-sexual after our first son was born, and I decided to stay anyway because you assured me that you engaged in such activity before we were married and not since?
- Could you hate me because I forgave you for sleeping in our bed with a man I considered a "family friend"?
- Could you hate me because I chose not to be abused and bullied by you during my pregnancy with our daughter and opted to leave you instead?
- Could you possibly hate me because I would not allow you to telephone me and tell me about your multitudinous affairs with gay men after you moved back to New Jersey?
- Could you hate me because I showed your mother the letter of confession you sent to me and she confirmed that I was the only girl you ever brought home and loved?
- Could you hate me because when I moved back to New Jersey you showed up at my parent's house with your lover in tow adorned with clogs, straw hat, and man purse and your secret was no longer a secret?
- Could you hate me because you still loved me?
- Could you hate me because I still loved you and wanted to get you back into my life with our children?
- Could you hate me because we slept together on many occasions even when you were in other relationships until I learned to stop wanting you unless you were free again?
- Do you hate me because you chose to be an absentee father because, according to you, "It's not conducive to my lifestyle."

- Do you hate me because I became a strong, independent single parent able to maintain our children despite your $20.00 per week per child for their entire childhood?
- Do you hate me for your last marriage choice even after we talked about getting back together? Do you remember telling me that you wondered if you had made the right decision as you came to get our children for a "dress up" party which really was a reception for your wedding that day? I found out you had done the deed when I got to the car and saw a bridal bouquet in your third wife's hand!

Did I make mistakes? Of course, I did. The biggest one I made was I did not believe the rumors about you before I fell in love with you. My biggest regret has been, and always will be, not going the distance with our marriage. I saw my parents fight, and I wanted no part of a life like that. Perhaps I was premature, but I was pregnant and hormonal at the time and you were acting insufferable, not remorseful or apologetic for cheating on me with a man!

What boggles my imagination is how you can say that you hate me when, every time we are in the same proximity, we laugh and joke with each other. Even our children have witnessed the cordiality between us. They have even teased about us getting back together if only we could get rid of your wife!

If anyone should have emoted hate, it quite possibly should be me!
- I should hate you for coming back from Vietnam with syphilis and not letting me know until after we got married to be told in a letter that I should go get checked out by a physician before I joined you in Colorado.
- I should hate you for trying to commit suicide when our son was three months old because you were too scared to tell me the truth about your sexuality.
- I should hate you for spreading lies that it was I who was gay and, therefore, the cause of the divorce.
- I should hate you for getting out of bed with me and going home with your lover right after we had made love.

- I should hate you for trying to take my children from me because your last wife could not reproduce.
- I should hate you for all the years you have been closeted and took no responsibility for the demise of our family.
- I should hate you for making me doubt my own femininity or ability to be a woman who could fully satisfy a man's sexual needs?

I could hate you for pulling our daughter into this matter. When I called you, I offered to be a sounding board for you if you needed a friend to help you through the grieving process. I even told you that it would only be between us that we talked. If you hated me so much, why did you return the phone call? Why weren't you man enough to tell me that you hate me and never want to hear my voice again?

I suppose that it is because of your own misery that you want to implant your infectious venom into my relationship with our daughter. I suspect that you have been unhappy for most of your life. How could you be happy when you can't be truthful to yourself or others?

I don't lay in judgment of you. I really pity you. You are so far afield that you don't even know when someone else really cares about your sorry behind! I invited you to stay with me for a brief change of scenery before you had to face the ordeal of getting rid of your wife's things.

I offered you my friendship and understanding. To learn that all you feel for me, as the mother of your three beautiful children who nearly died twice in childbirth, is hatred is mortifying to say the least.

After all the messes you caused in my life, I have never hated you. I have prayed for you, dreamed about you, worried about you, and reached out to you for more than 48 years. And for the record, I was the one who told our son to go and stay with you after your wife died because I feared you may hurt yourself or revert back to your old habits. And to your insufferable credit, you maligned him and his intention to be there for you in your time of need. You really are a bitch after all!

You have continued to keep your children at arm's length. You have done likewise with your grandchildren. You are a person stuck in your past, full of vengefulness, unforgiving, and an erasable sense of unrighteous indignation.

I am stuck in my ways also. I refuse to treat people unlike I want to be treated. I am still a caring and affectionate person. I still look for the good in everybody. Maybe it is my naiveté that I refuse to give up. To be or do otherwise would diminish the person God created me to be.

Now having said all I think I need to say on the matter, I close with these words I have used with you in the past: Take care of yourself. That is the only thing you are good at doing.

I am finally ready to close this chapter of my life. Life is too short to waste it on the undeserved. I will continue to love you because my God tells me so. You will have to answer to Him for your behavior. Peace out!   LSJ 6/8/14

(1)Oxford University Press © 2014   (2) Merriam-Webster, Inc. © 2014
(3)Freud, S. The instincts and their vicissitudes. Reber, A. S. & Reber, E © 1915 (4)The Penguin dictionary of psychology. New York: Penguin Books © 2002. (5)Macmillan Publishers Limited © 2009-2014

EMOTIONAL BARRICADE

There's a wall.
Is it going up or coming down brick by brick?
There's a fence between us.
Do we straddle it or jump over it?
Limbo is a dance, not a place either of us want to be
Where do we go from here?
Is there reason to steadily move forward,
Or shall we stand still
In the tracks of uncertainty or indecision?
What kind of future do you see?
What do your guts tell you?
Are we in it together?
You said you can't say anything you can't mean,
But what exactly does that mean?

Life is a progression of trials and errors –
Getting up and falling down again,
Falling in and out of love –
Happiness and sadness –
Shedding tears of joy and grief.
That's what it's all about!

We must glean what little satisfaction we can
While time is still on our side.
Tomorrow is not promised.
Let us make the most of today,
Say all that we would want to have said
As if time had run out –
Having no regrets.
Forget all of the " I should have(s)"
And "I could have(s)."
Just do it!
What do you have to lose?
EVERYTHING if you aren't careful!

Patricia Ann Woolfork

REQUIEM FOR A DISGRUNTLED HOUSEWIFE

The vows have barely left our lips,
but the honeymoon seems over.
You come in from work without even asking
how my day has been or
giving me a simple kiss on the cheek.
I've labored long over a hearty meal,
prepared with love,
longing for your attention,
a little romantic dinner by candlelight,
Only to hear,
"I'm going to watch a little TV in the den."

I've washed and ever so gently folded
your undershirts and shorts,
paired your elastic-stretched socks, and
tucked them away in drawers ever so organized
without so much as "thank you."

I long to get even one long-stemmed rose,
the simple "Hallmark" card that says
how much you appreciate me,
how much you love me,
how much I mean to you, and
how happy marrying me has made you.

However, I am locked in some dream state –
of broken promises, unfulfilled wishes,
dashed dreams and tormented longings.
I ask myself, "Why did this man marry me?"
"Am I still just a convenience,
a staple like a roll of toilet tissue,
to be used only when necessary?"

Savoring Eden

I lay awake at night and wonder if
I have been a fool
Have I been fooled
by the hype –
the tears
the pleadings for yet another chance?
My heart yearns to be optimistic,
but my mind struggles with my reality.

I have married a man
who'd rather live like a single man,
wants to be bothered only
when he wants to be bothered,
make love only when
he wants to make what . . .?
A man who only goes out as a couple
only after much cajoling.
A man who'd rather spend time with
the boys on a nightly basis
than come home to a loving,
warm, compassionate woman –
the one he claimed he longed for
in the first place.

I am stuck in a quagmire of indecision.
My life thus far has been riddled
with despair and longing.
Am I too old to continue on a path
that my heart feels
is leading to more disappointment?
I know that I deserve better!
I am talented.
I am loving and lovable.
I am supportive and caring.
I am a romantic at heart, and
extremely sexual if given the time of day!

Patricia Ann Woolfork

I am at a point where
I am finding it difficult to even like this man.
I am a glass
brimming to overflow with resentment.
I grow intolerant with each passing day
that I am –
Ignored,
Disrespected,
Discounted, and
Dismissed!

How long . . .
will I accept this travesty,
enable this man to dishonor me,
break his promises and vows to this union?
This marriage is becoming
a continuous "Saturday Night Live" –
a farce of gargantuan proportions!
How long . . .
will I keep up the façade,
keep the secret of unhappiness and
disappointment,
protect the image of newlywed bliss?

How long can I go on . . .
without reaching the precipice
of emotional suicide?
I feel like I am at the edge –
One more criticism,
One more unkind remark,
One more, "You're just like my mother,"
One more story about his daughter's mother,
One more story about his ex-wife, and
how he tried to save her from her reputation –

Savoring Eden

One more minute . . .
that I have to watch him
put that bottle of E&J and Budweiser to his lips –
One more day . . .
that I have to smell the cigarettes
and liquor on his breath –
One more weekend alone
even when he's home –
One more second . . .
of trying to figure out which way
his mood swing is going to take him –
One more lie –
One more promise that it won't happen again –
One more complaint –
One more utterance of the word, "FUCK!!"

And let me not forget the slap –
The punch to the back of my head,
The names . . .
"Cunt," "Bitch," Cocksucker," and "Whore,"
that spouted so profusely
out of that drunken mouth of yours!
God help me,
But a bullet in my brain
would be more humane!

I am becoming joyless.
I want my smiles to return.
I want my heat to resurface.
I want my happiness
to speak volumes to the universe.
I want a marriage that is real and satisfying.
I want my husband
to be whole in mind and body.
I want my husband
to take care of me like I take care of him.
I want passion, fire, and unbridled sex!

Patricia Ann Woolfork

I want the happy ever after.
I want the prince even if his armor is tarnished.
I want the little castle to be our sanctuary
against the cold, cruel world outside.

I want to be held
just because he loves me and it feels good.
I want to be told
I am loved without intercourse.
I want
a kiss good-bye and a kiss hello.
I want to
watch TV in his embrace,
take walks holding hands,
share a picnic in the park, and
snuggle in front of the fireplace.

I want the world to know
he's made a wise decision
in taking me as his bride.
I want to know
he has no regrets with having done so.
I want to be spontaneous.
I want to laugh and cry with ecstasy
at how well my life has turned out.

I want my past to remain in the past.
I want my life
to have substance, purpose, and meaning.
I want my legacy to be that of a good:
Mother,
Grandmother,
Daughter,
Friend,
Lover,
Teacher,
Student,
Listener,
Decorator,

Savoring Eden

Writer,
Cook,
Faithful companion –
A genuinely good person.

I am all of that
With or without a husband,
Preferably with,
But,
It's up to ME now!

Dedicated to EAG

Patricia Ann Woolfork

DEAR JIM,

I just wanted to touch base since we have not spoken
For nearly a month since I invited you to the concert.
Although you told me we would get together during
The Xmas holidays by going to your extended family
And friends on Xmas Day,
I heard nothing from you –
Not even that your plans had changed, or
You weren't up to company, whatever.

I feel not only disappointed, but also offended
By your lack of consideration for my feelings.
I am grieving every bit as hard as you are
Since the recent loss of my 57-year friendship with LaVonne,
But I found the time to reach out to you and
Include you in something special to me.
I thought we had a lovely time, and
I was happy not to have to go alone
As I do to most things.
Then you reverted to your habit of non-communication.
I find this to be unacceptable behavior
As well as downright rude!

I offered you my friendship that September morning
Out of compassion for the loss of your wife, but
I don't know if you really want it or
If you know how to be my friend.
I have yet to get a call from you in the New Year.

Unless there has been another death in your family
As I have in mine (four more to be exact in one month),
Had a bad accident, a serious illness, or
Your fingers are broken and your mouth sewn shut,
I cannot find an acceptable, excusable reason
For this lack of manners.
You asked me not to ignore you and to forgive you

Savoring Eden

For your shortcomings,
So here I am – I am not ignoring you.
I am calling you out for them!

A real friend would not
Let you get away with this shitty behavior.
I may not be your friend, but I am real!
I have a heart and soul that has been stricken with heartbreak,
And I refuse to let my spirit be crushed, too,
With broken promises and inconsideration.

LaVonne is irreplaceable, as is your wife, but
She did teach me what being a friend should look like
And feel like – and
So far this isn't it!

I do hope that you will give me the courtesy
Of a verbal response
Since I already told you how I feel about texting.
In my heart, though, I don't expect to hear from you,
But my hope is that, in this instance, I am incorrect.

The ball is in your court.
It is up to you to decide if you want to keep it in play.
Be well.
Be healthy.
Be blessed.

Always,

IF THE SHOE FITS

Just a quick note to someone I recently offered friendship: The truth is sometimes painful. It is, however, still the truth. I am sorry you could not handle being called out for your lack of common courtesy and that you did not have the strength of character to apologize or acknowledge your lack of decorum. If you weren't a highly educated person, I might have been able to overlook your "bitch-ass" move to "unfriend" me instead of pick up the phone and address me like the man you are supposed to be.

I am not, now or ever have been, desperate. Guilty of not being able to read a phony, yes! Let us not get it twisted—you were not a friend. You were someone I felt compassion for and offered you the possibility of friendship because of your loss.

Since I lost my best friend, LaVonne, two days before Thanksgiving, I thought it would have been nice to be around someone else who understands the devastation that occurs to one's daily existence. She taught me what real friendship was, what it should look like, and how it should make you feel. Alas, you weren't even close!

I hope the next person who crosses your path fares better than I did. In fact, I hope you refrain from making new acquaintances until you are more emotionally stable. I had no hidden agenda, was not looking for romance or intimacy—just someone to talk to, laugh with, and maybe share a meal or a movie, learn more about the city, etc., and give you someone you could talk to while you are grieving.

I just wanted you to know that you hurt me for no excusable reason. You asked me to spend the holidays with you and your friends (your idea and suggestion not mine), and you never showed up or called—not even a Happy New Year!

This is a new year. It is a time for do overs and renewals. I intend to make the most of my new opportunity to improve myself and enhance my life. I will not change my ability to display empathy, sympathy, compassion, or friendliness to others.

I am a survivor and one who thrives. My God will supply all of my needs. He will open a new door when one closes. He will get me through my grief and loneliness. He will get me prepared for all the many blessings He has coming my way.

With that said, I wish you well and that your pain subsides in due course, and that you remember to treat others as you would want to be treated.

Sincerely,

TICK TOCK

It's 4:45 A.M. and I can't sleep.
I'm lying here wondering, "What the hell am I doing?"
Why am I allowing myself to feel downhearted?
Why am I allowing myself to feel abused, taken for granted?
Am I wearing my heart on my shoulder –
Like some chip to be knocked off at will?
Is there a tattoo across my forehead that reads:
I will accept whatever gets dished out?

Okay, I know that sounds a bit fucked up,
But I've waited since 10:46 A.M. yesterday
To share a moment in time with you.
I called to say that I woke up aching for you again
And to ask you what you were going to do about it?
I watched the minutes tick past
As I waited for you to return my call
So I could hear that sexy laugh when I described
All the things I wanted to do that lean, chocolate body.

You see,
You are more than an object for my pleasure.
I want you not out of desperation,
But out of an ever-increasing affection.
But now I ask myself, as the tears slowly slide down
My plump cheeks that you love so much to tweak,
Am I playing some kind of dangerous game
With my heart and my mind?
One I may never win with you
Because we are unequally matched
And you have all of the winning moves?

Savoring Eden

I taste the salt of my tears and reflect on the past –
All of the hurts, the fears and triumphs.
I blink away the tears for our future
Which I hold in my mind's eye
Through which each crystal drop gets blurred
Like those tiny words we try to read on the medicine bottle.

Am I treading on old pavement,
On roads I've traversed before?
Am I clutching to the crumbs of life
Like ever so many sidewalk pigeons,
Grateful for whatever gets tossed my way?

I THINK NOT!
You see, I am no longer a crumb snatcher!
I am like an eagle or any other creature of majesty.
I refuse to be devalued.
It is my time to soar!
TICK TOCK

It is time to love myself first and then others.
It is time to get what I want, but most of all,
What I need
To feel accomplished, complete, satisfied and content.
I am no longer complacent or compromised, nor
Full of regret, needy, nor desperate.
Knowing when to let go and when to continue holding on,
I am true to myself at last!
I will acknowledge my pain and its cause
And no longer be held prisoner by it.

TICK TOCK
It's 6:15 A.M. and I still can't sleep
But my tears have dried
And I wait to greet the new day
With a new, improved me!
I WRITE, THEREFORE, I AM

I Wanted to Believe

I wanted to believe.
I tried to conceive of the idea that for once
Someone told the truth.
I wanted to believe.
I tried to conceive the notion that
I really could be a part of your life.
I wanted to believe.
I tried to conceive the possibility that
What I desire can be achieved.
I wanted to believe that
You really were falling in love with me,
With all that those words can convey.
I wanted to believe that
I could be more than a conquest, a trophy to be won.

I wanted to believe the hype,
Alas, all of the lies.
I tried to conceive within my heart and mind
That you could really make love with me,
Not FUCK me –
Then I could forget all of the other lies you told.
I wanted to believe that you could be –
Punctual –
Considerate –
A man of your word.
Alas,
I WANTED TO BELIEVE!

A Moment

I watched your hair blow in the wind
As your head rested upon my knee.
I saw the sunlight in your eyes
As you gazed back at me.
It was such beauty to behold –
Your warmth, so close, so near.
Why couldn't it last beyond a day
Before it disappeared?

I watched as your insecurity . . .
Tossed us from ecstasy back into reality
Deny dreams,
Strip away desires
Tease with overtures of delight
Then snatch possibilities away.
It told you over and over again
"You do not deserve."
And for a moment . . .
"Yes you can."

I ask . . .
Can joy be found for longer than a moment?
Security for more than an hour?
A lover for more than a night?
Love for a lifetime?

You were my fantasy fulfilled,
The joy I long hoped for.
Alas,
You were but a mirage,
A moment,
Nothing more.

REGRET

It's times like these
That makes my love for you turn into hatred and despair.
I hate the way you make me long for you.
I hate the way you make me feel unimportant to you.
I hate the way I've become emotionally connected to you.
You hurt me whether you realized you were doing it or not.
The pain pierced right through my heart
And left a gaping hole where all of my love for you resides.
I gave you all of me unreservedly.
I gave you my love,
My body,
My home,
My family,
My support.
I've been there for you.
Why couldn't you be there for me?
Was it too much that I let you know that I missed you,
That I wanted to spend quality time with you?
It pains me that I believed you.
I thought you really did want a commitment.

Do you see the spots on this page?
They are the remains of the tears
I shed for you yesterday.

SATURDAY NIGHT

Idle chatter fills the air.
Ice hits glass,
Clink, clink.
Lonely people gather for iced cold comfort.
Chilled drinks uncover
Emotions buried beneath layers and layers of denial.
Laughter is superficial.
Games played to the hilt.
Lies told.
Lies believed.
There's a momentary lapse in the loneliness.
Lights are dim and hope is bright.
Will I?
Will I find love tonight?

BALANCING ACT

It's an amazing thing
This thing called balance.
Amazing that two people,
Identical in every way but one,
Can be so transformed by it.

Men most often say exactly what they mean.
Yet, women never clearly hear what is said to them.
Our logical mind is often unable to identify
That fine line between what is emotion and what is reality.

When a man says,
"I don't want to say anything I don't mean",
A woman interprets it as "but I will love you someday".
When a man says,
"I don't want to let anything interfere with my career",
A woman supposes
That does not include his relationship with her.
When a man says, "I'll call you later",
A woman believes in his honesty.

When a man makes love to a woman,
It is often simply a release of tension –
A natural function –
A feel good for the moment.

When a woman makes love to a man,
It most often means –
Commitment of mind, body, soul, and spirit –
A gift from God.

Savoring Eden

She envisions –
Tomorrow and tomorrows –
Sunrise and sunset together –
Loving embraces –
Passionate kisses –
Wholeness.

Where, alas, does balance play its part?
Could it be the balance of Nature
For man to procreate and
Woman to nurture?
Man to flee and
Woman to secure a nest?
Sounds more like imbalance,
Doesn't it?

We each have the same hormones,
But it's the balance of same
That makes us want what we cannot have –
Have what we do not want –
And never know the difference.

THE JOURNEY

My inspiration for writing comes from the great Maya Angelou. When I first started this journey, I was happy to learn that she was one of our elders. That is why Sacred Spirit Gateway spoke to me. She had a book entitled, "Won't Take Nothing for My Journey Now." This further led me to write about my amazing Journey to Wellness as a Sacred Medicine Woman, I might add. (LOL)

When I came to my first Day of Transformation on November 6, 2010, I was broken in mind, body, and spirit. I thought I needed to take desperate measures if I was to survive. And so, desperate, I came to hold on tightly to the doorknob of opportunity which had become opened to me by invitation by Queen Afua herself.

When I envisioned how I would incorporate "Sacred Word" in this presentation the theme of butterflies kept coming into my mind's eye. Before it becomes the beautiful specimen we all know and love to observe . . . a transformation must take place. It begins as a creepy, crawling, slow-moving, fat and furry caterpillar. Sure it has pretty markings and is soft and furry and soft to the touch but be honest, no one wants to stay a caterpillar.

As time goes by, the caterpillar goes through a metamorphosis. It spins a tight cocoon around itself and attaches itself to a limb on a tree or bush. Within days of that first intervention, I was wound up tightly in the cocoon of fasting and breathing, crying and meditating, trying to do yoga poses, living without my barbeque ribs and steak!

Queen Afua was my cocoon. She lovingly guided me and encouraged me. She has allowed me to use my divine sacred word ability to transform some of her own words for our SMW Training. I was blessed to assist her in the preparation of her newest book, Man, Heal Thyself: A 14 Day Guide to Mind, Body, and Spirit Wellness.

Back to the butterfly—while in the cocoon, away from prying eyes, it goes through all kinds of changes, and as if that wasn't hard enough in itself, it has to battle to break out of the cocoon. The process can't be hastened in anyway. In other words, it's not a quick fix. Really is anything in the life worth having ever appreciated if it is just given to us? It was in the darkness of the cocoon, that I and my other sacred sisters purged and meditated and struggled to eat right, get ourselves to classes, be called "weird" by our peers, not be supported by our significant others, deal with other people's opinions, struggle with a bad economy, have our electricity turned off, deal with broken down automobiles, and battle.

My struggle in that cocoon wasn't just physical. There were financial dilemmas one right after another—no oil, no heat, frozen and broken water pipes—inability to buy product or Gateway aids. And let's not forget the snowstorms. But through the struggle I held true to my path. My process could not be hurried.

There were others watching me to witness either my success or my failure. There were others to be talked to about my historic journey. There were my new-found sisters to share experiences with, to cry with, to laugh with, to dance with, and to bond with. Such has been the case in my Sacred Medicine Woman Journey.

Fat, though not furry, I arrived, slow-moving, rarely feeling appreciated—having yet to acknowledge my real purpose in life. However, within a 12-week journey, I lost 15 lbs. My skin had a glow that even my physician made comment. My spirit has been lightened. My words have healing powers. I have learned how to use my Sacred Word to encourage not only myself but others as well.

After this caterpillar spends time in this state of suspended animation, the secret of the cocoon is revealed—A BEAUTIFUL, MAJESTIC BUTTERFLY! Songs have been written about it, gardens have been especially designed for them so we can enjoy watching the butterfly fly from bloom to bloom.

However, before the butterfly can take flight, its wings must dry out from the moisture of the cocoon. Such has been my experience. Time is needed to reprogram from the negative practices of eating dairy, white sugar, processed foods, having poisonous relationships, bad attitudes, and being unrepentant and unforgiving. I am a work in progress. I have made some slips and have some do-overs to do.

I am not quite ready to take flight, but I am now using my expert cooking skills on a higher level. I am becoming a kitchen chemist, a recipe magician—I can make chia, flaxseed, and other healthy ingredients undetectable. My vegetable, tofu, and dessert dishes are slamming! My wings are brightly colored in the colors of faith, hope, endurance, strength, peace and love as I eagerly await my lift off!

THE PERSONAL AD

The ad read: 45 SBPM ISO SW/H/Asian/F 25-35 for LTR.
Translation: 45 year- old, Single Black Professional Male
In search of Single White, Hispanic or Asian Female age 25-35
for long term relationship.

What's the matter "Broth a?"
Or shall I say, "Brother?"
Do you know what you are missing?
I've got brains, body and soul.
I, too, have been through the struggle,
And I have come out victorious.

But, you'll never know how –
We can strengthen each other –
Continue our race –
Fortify our defenses because –
You don't have the common sense
To be in search of me –
A Single 45-year-old
Educated
Professional
Independent
African-American Goddess!
Your loss!

Patricia Ann Woolfork

THE JOURNEY OF A SACRED WOMAN

Sacred Woman in the making
Sacred Woman shaking with anticipation
Sacred Woman awakening
To all the possibilities that lie ahead.
Sacred Woman quaking in my shoes
As I stand before you today.

Sacred Medicine Woman in training
Sacred Medicine Woman gaining
Knowledge and confidence
In my ability to help others transform their lives to wellness.
Sacred Woman grateful,
Sacred Woman ever faithful in my journey.

Like a butterfly, I am being transformed.
I started out as a caterpillar – slowly moving along
Inch by inch I dragged my heavy little body toward
My juice, My tonic – My herbal life, oh yum!
Toward my yoga dance, ouch! –
Toward my fresh steamed veggies
Away from my spareribs, potato chips, and Good & Plenty
Toward the wellness of my mind, body and my spirit.

My transformation continued as I read, meditated,
Listened to my inner voice
Believed in my healing
Shared my experience with friends and family alike
Prepared new recipes in my wellness kitchen
Watched as nearly 15 lbs dropped from my body.

Cocooned at last away from prying eyes,
I was guided, comforted, supported, and encouraged
By Queen Afua herself and my new
Sacred Medicine Woman sisters.
There were challenges that had to be dealt with

Savoring Eden

While in the cocoon
That could have discouraged all of us from our course.
Yet we remain victorious in our quest
To become Sacred Medicine Women in the making –
Taking on the responsibility to lead others
To their Divine Mind, Body, and Spiritual Wellness.

So thus we emerge today from our respective cocoons
Beautiful butterflies all –
Ready to take flight to spread the news
That we have the power to heal ourselves
And others from disease –
Through knowledge and commitment to the well-being
Of ourselves and our families,
Our communities and our world!

Patricia Ann Woolfork

IF MY VAGINA COULD TALK, WHAT WOULD SHE SAY?*

She would say, "Stop!" "Cease!" and "Desist!" She would utter a blood curdling scream to get you to pay attention! She would tell you that she was molested and physically abused as a child by her father who took her virginity and by a first cousin she trusted. She would tell you that she was raped as an adult by another cousin as her children lay sleeping near her and sexually assaulted by a date. She would tell you that she has been torn, cut, abused, used, nearly bled to death in childbirth and had her womb removed.

She would say, "I have been devalued and disrespected by my guardian and taken advantage of by countless unworthy partners and cheated on and physically, verbally, and emotionally abused by those who vowed to love and protect me 'til death do us part."

She would say, "I have been promiscuous—looking for love in all the wrong places—for all the wrong reasons." I have been cheated on, brutally penetrated, have suffered physical, emotional, and psychic pain and trauma."

She would say, "I know I deserve better. I am finally taking care of myself. I am picky—not just anybody can enter into my golden gates. I am nearly new again with inactivity."

She would say, "My guilt has subsided. My childhood trauma was not my fault. My adult decisions were faulty and misguided, but they were the result of former experiences. I know better now. I know I am worthy of a divine mate and real love and affection. I am older and wiser." She would say, "I still have longing, but I am in control! I am no longer desperate. I don't need to be a people pleaser. I don't have to do anything that makes me uncomfortable. I don't have to please anyone but myself!"

She would say, "I am healthy emotionally and physically. I am warm, wet, vibrant, and tight! I am ready to sing a new song of freedom, forgiveness, joy, peace and wholeness for and to myself!"

This poem and the ones entitled, "The Journey", and "Sacred Medicine Woman in the Making" were assignments I had to write as part of a 13-week workshop that I did back in 2011 for mind, body, and spiritual renewal. I was learning how to meditate, eat a more vegan diet, use herbs, learn how to prepare raw foods and juices, and attempt to do yoga according to African ancestral customs and rituals.

AM I READY?

Arms entangled
Web of limbs enfold
Terror creeps in on little padded feet.
Space encroached upon
Breath caught in midair.
Heartbeat goes rat-tat-tat-tat
Perspiration is misty.
Anxiety is mounting.
Am I ready for COMMITMENT?

A Portrait of Grieving and Loss

A PORTRAIT OF GRIEVING AND LOSS

Loss is something we all experience. How we handle it is different for each individual. It is a state of being that we cannot escape. Losing my best friend was the most profound loss I have ever experienced. I have shed tears over many friends and family members over the years, but with this one, it was like a piece of my soul was ripped out. I chose to write it out.

I have lost friends, relationships, the death of my childhood innocence, and so much more. God gave me a gift that allows me to be able to express my emotions through poetry and prose which has enabled me to find beauty for my ashes, and help others find their words, too.

My goal is to both bring comfort and the knowledge that we are not alone in this shared human experience of love, loss, grief, and survival—one day at a time.

MY THERAPIST

I watch him wondering
What does he think of me?
Is he sincerely interested
In my recovery from depression?
Does he really believe in my talent?
Can he see the big picture?
Where does he think I will go from here?
Does he really believe in my potential,
Or
Is this just his job – a job – NEXT?

My intuition tells me that he is the real deal
Led by Christian principle to say and to do
The ethical, truthful thing –
Lead me as Jesus would do –
Build me up but,
Always tell me the truth, and
Help me see my own truth in order to
Guide me toward
The next step to my emotional healing.
I must
Trust that my Creator has guided me
To be in this place
At this particular time
With this particular person
For His purpose as He has always done.
I must believe in myself and be open to those,
I truly believe, He has led into my path.
It was I who didn't always watch out
And listen to Him.
My way has often been the wrong way, but
I am in a continual state of metamorphosis, and
I am woman enough to admit it.

The Backstory

Dedicated to J. Thomas Sandy, PsyD

I had been going to counselling on a weekly basis when I lived in New Jersey, which fortunately had started before LaVonne was diagnosed with Breast Cancer. I don't think I could even bring myself to write at that time. I would take her for her treatments every two weeks, but I would stay in my bed for those two weeks, cussing God for taking my friend, or so I thought.

I would have to keep a brave face, never say anything discouraging, or talk about my feelings or my grief to her or her family. I had to be the strong one for everybody else. I knew her longer than her own household.

I would take her for her chemo, and the next day I would pick her up to take her for her shot which would prevent infections. Then I would go back to bed. We would talk on the phone, but I would hide my anguish. That went on until her cancer went in remission, which lasted for five years, and it was not the cause of her untimely death.

I had moved to Alabama in 2012, and I still had no therapist. It was either, my insurance would not cover it, or copay that I could not afford. Well, three weeks before LaVonne died, I finally found Dr. Sandy. I was able to tell him about LaVonne and tell LaVonne about him. We were a perfect team. They each were okay with the match.

Everything is in God's timing. He knew when and who to put in my path for the most major loss in my lifetime. I lost the only person who, I knew for a certainty, loved me unconditionally as much as I loved her. It was such a shock to lose her after all we had been through together with the cancer, and there was nothing I could do about it 1,000 miles away.

It has been Dr. Sandy that has guided me toward keeping my sanity in spite of my grief, loneliness, and temporary hopelessness. Only God could make this happen. I have been so blessed. It was Dr. Sandy who listened to me sob when I could not talk in a session. It was Dr. Sandy that made me pick up my pen and express these emotions. It was even Dr. Sandy who listened to the eulogy I had to prepare for LaVonne's funeral.

I really don't know how I made it through that experience without a total meltdown! Yes, I do—only God! It was Dr. Sandy who helped me pick up the pieces of my broken heart every week after I got back from the funeral, but it was God that gave him to me for that purpose. It was God that made me open up my fragile heart to someone I could entrust it to without hesitation,

Here we are almost four years later, and I am writing in my manuscript, about to be published. There is no one else more deserving of my gratitude and appreciation. So I honor you on this page as a token of my never-ending admiration of the Christian principles you display on a weekly basis, and for your truthfulness, honesty, cheerleading, firmness, objectivity, kindness, and generosity.

Forever grateful,

Patricia Ann Woolfork
8/16/18

Patricia Ann Woolfork

WHEN THE WAILING STOPPED

November 26, 2014   4:00 A.M. –

My beautiful friend, LaVonne
How will I live without you in my life?
You have been an integral part of it for nearly fifty years!
How will I go through a day, a week,
Without talking to you on the phone,
Making you laugh – you, hearing my tears?
How will a memory not cause a tear to slide down my face?

I cried for you today –
No, I WAILED!
So overcome with grief – disbelief
Still not knowing WHY??
We just spent several hours on the phone yesterday,
Laughing,
Joking,
Sharing milestones,
Speaking of grandchildren.

You called me your sister/friend –
More than friends –
SOUL Sisters!
We loved unconditionally,
With whole hearts,
Never holding back through the good times and the bad.

How could you kick cancer in the butt
(6 years cancer free), and
Be taken out like this – without warning?
Thanksgiving week – déjà vu
(You got the diagnosis during Thanksgiving week)

How can I never hear your voice again?
How will I ever enjoy
A steak, sushi, Jimmy Buffs, corned beef, and

Savoring Eden

Your rutabagas without you –
Not to mention our crab feast!

You were the most uplifting, positive, inspirational,
Tell me like it is person,
I have ever believed and trusted implicitly.

Oh, how I wanted to be with you two weeks ago, but
Remember, you said you wanted me to come
When we could run to our old stomping grounds, and
You could fully enjoy the visit?

How will my Alabama neighbors never get to meet
The friend I raved about sooooo much?
How can I endure not having you to LOVE me?
You have been my constant, consistent,
Unconditional,
Soul companion!
Who will be my beneficiary now?

We'd go to school together,
Eat lunch together,
Have most classes together,
Ride the bus back home together, and
Still get on the phone for a couple of hours
Every single day!

You taught me how to sew, knit and crochet.
You taught me what friendship means.
Oh, how you would get me about using the word "friend"
Too loosely, too prematurely!
Who else would love Patches more than you?
Who will I trust with my secrets and my vulnerabilities?

I MISS YOU ALREADY!!!!!

I have cried every minute since I heard the news –
Ten hours and counting . . .
ALONE – without you to comfort me.

ALONE – unable to comfort our family back home.
I guess my timing was finally on time with finding a therapist.
You timed this just right –
I go to see him later this morning instead of Friday
Because of THANKSGIVING!

How will Benji get comfortable at night
Without you as his pillow?
I was happy that you got to enjoy being a grandmother.
I always said that I wanted to be one of your animals,
But that care and affection pales in comparison
To the attention that Angelica and Blake received!
Wasn't it GREAT?

I should not be sad
Because you had an exemplary life –
A loving, dutiful, adoring and devoted husband,
Two beautiful adoring and doting children and
Me! (smile)
And, you shared them with me.

I will think of you every time I see an elephant,
Wear something pink,
Remember your smile and your laughter.
I found five "friendship" cards yesterday and said,
"I need to send these to LaVonne."
Were you watching me read them?
Were you already gone?

I will not let you down my dear friend.
I will continue to make you proud of me.
Your love was not wasted on me!
Every piece of prose I write in the future
Will be dedicated to you.
Tell Butch "hello."
Mommy Peaches is waiting, and
Daddy Clarence remembers his little girl again!
Maybe Rasheema
Will sing to you with her ever angelic voice.

Savoring Eden

Tell her I miss her, too.
Oooooo, don't forget Bernie –
Bet he still thinks he's fine!
Evelyn is probably grinning as I write these lines, and
Bob and Dot are there, too.

If you didn't suffer, I am somewhat pacified,
You deserved a serene exit –
Halo and golden-tipped wings –
Just because you loved me in spite of myself –
Sometimes,
Even more than I was capable of loving me.

My friend,
My mentor,
My cheerleader,
My counselor,
My confidant,
My little sister – I had you by 18 days!

Every time I sit in this recliner and
Look at the room you said I made beautiful,
I will share a moment with you.
I will imagine you talking to me
As the fire flickers in the fireplace, and
As I watch the lights twinkle of the every season tree.

Every time I see a beautiful Alabama sky or sunset –
I will see it through your eyes and smile.
You sent me here to be in a better place
Even if it was without you –
Never a selfish bone in your body!
They say that death comes in threes –
Why did you have to take your turn right now?
We had so much left to do together.

You knew me better than I know myself.
You know I got mad at HIM again!
I asked, "What lesson do I still need to learn?"

I didn't cuss HIM out this time.
I will wait on HIM . . . .
To provide me a safe place,
To provide all my needs,
To heal my physical and mental anguish –
To make me more like you in
Gentility,
Gentleness,
Kindness,
Patience,
Long-Suffering and Loyalty.
I MISS YOU!!!!!!!!!!

Help me LORD,
To make it through this night and
Into dawn's early light!
Rest my precious.
Take a load off.
You ran a fine race.
We'll catch up soon.
Longevity is over-rated,
BUT YOU ARE GONE TOO SOON!
I will love you with every breath I will take
From this day forward until my last.
WE ALL MISS YOU!
I will do my best to comfort ALL that we loved dearly.

Always your devoted sister/friend, Patricia Ann

Sharing My Grief with My Facebook Friends

Wednesday 12:26 AM – November 26. 2014
MY BEST AND DEAREST MOST CHERISHED SISTER/FRIEND. . . I MISS YOU ALREADY. Who will love me more than you have all these many years? I will try to not be mad at HIM too long. I know you got those gold tips on your wings last night, but my heart is breaking!

Wednesday 12:54 AM –
My best friend has left me, and I am heartbroken. My strength comes from the knowledge that she truly loved me unconditionally as I her.

My love and sympathy to out to Leroy, Roy, Shara, Alexis, Mike, Angelica, Blake and all the extended family that counted me as one of their own.

Sister/Friend, I am still going to wear your ear out every day until we meet again. Your love will sustain us all. We will be there for each other because that is what I know you expect of us. LOVE YOU SOOOOO MUCH.

I am so happy that we ended each conversation with "I love you." Wish I had a chance yesterday. Golden tips, right? XOXO to infinity.

Thanksgiving Day 7:04 AM –
I lost my best friend in the whole world on Tuesday, LaVonne Marie Adams-Hopkins. I am DEVASTATED! We have known each other since 3rd grade and became best friends in 9th grade. She was my sister, confidant, cheerleader, and my soul.

I finally know what it means to wail in grief! Went to pick up the phone and call her last night because I forgot to tell her something. Just when I think I have no tears left, they roll again.

This is the greatest loss of my life. We were Celie without Nettie and vice versa. We never ended a conversation without reaffirming our love for each other. How will I endure never hearing her voice or her laugh again? MY HEART IS RIPPING, TORN, MUCH MORE THAN BREAKING!

I had her laughing on Monday that if there is a heaven, she is going to have a jeweled halo and her wings are going to be tipped in gold for putting up with me and loving me unconditionally for more than 50 years. And now, she has them both, I suppose—well earned.

My friend taught me what friendship means and would take me to task about using the word too frequently or prematurely on new people that were only acquaintances.

LaVonne was a most caring, patient, compassionate, loving and loyal friend anyone would be fortunate enough to get into her inner circle. What a privilege to be her BEST FRIEND—besides her husband and kids, and grandchildren, of course, but I KNEW HER LONGER!

In spite of my grief, I am happy about a few things: She had the best husband, the most attentive and adoring children, she got to be a doting and devoted grandmother, and she knew that she was loved and appreciated, and she shared them and all that love with me.

LORD, give us the strength needed to get through this monumental change in our daily existence. Let us continue to support each other in our sorrow and make our bond stronger. Protect our hearts and health and send your grace to protect us in our travel from near and far to make tribute to our most beloved LaVonne.

Rest darling girl. I am making my way to you. I know HE will provide the way. You can count on me to be there for those you loved the most. I will find the strength to be strong for them. You know that, right?

7:27 A.M. –
I am an only child, and LaVonne was my sister/friend. I am 1,000 miles away and don't know how I am getting back to NJ but will crawl if I have to in order to show my support. Plus I need to be able to share what I am feeling.

Got 2 hours sleep since 3:00 AM Tuesday, and as soon as my eyes opened, the tears started to slide. I am here alone with no one to talk to but my cat. I wish someone was here to wrap their arms around me so I could feel safe enough to let go. I am afraid I will start wailing again like I did after I hung up the phone after her husband told me that we had lost her. I stayed on the floor for nearly four hours rocking and wailing. Good thing my neighbor is nearly deaf!

7:56 A.M. – MY BEST FRIEND, rest until we meet again, I am still going to talk to you every day or write a poem and read it out loud for you to critique. Oh, how profoundly I miss you!
Go ahead . . . tell me to get a grip! (smile)

8:20 A.M. – I am sitting here reading our text messages – laughing and crying.

12:43 P.M. – (responding to my FB friends) I am happy I was able to touch your heart. I want everyone to know how dear and special LaVonne was to everyone whose life she touched. We had a special place in each other's heart.

November 30 –
My best friend, LaVonne Marie Adams-Hopkins funeral service will begin at noon, Friday, December 5, 2014, with viewing from 12-1p.m. and service at 1:00 p.m. at:
Woody Home for Services
163 Oakwood Avenue
Orange, NJ 07050

December 11 –
Food for thought – Thought I would have my best friend always, but now she is gone to that higher plain. I miss her all the same.

December 22. 2014 –
My newest angel, LaVonne Marie Adams-Hopkins, joins Rasheema, Bob and Dot, Butch, and my nephew, Bernie, and "My Mommy", Evelyn, and my aunt Geraldine – I'd say that's a pretty good watch team! Miss you all.

The Eulogy was compiled of these postings and other memories

I FEEL YOU

Although not driven to spontaneous tears
    This time
        As I step into the house where you once lived.
I Feel You . . .
    Within these walls.
I See You . . .
    In the bric-a-brac, the lacy curtains –
        In your cats' eyes.
I Feel You . . .
    When I see your handwriting on a left behind note –
        The occasional recipe.
I Hear You . . .
    In the many conversations we shared
    Both here and on the phone
        That have formed fond memories and
            Play loops within my heart and brain.
I Feel You . . .
    In the comfort of occupying a space
        Where you once stood.
I Feel You . . .
    When I witness your creative genius
        In the prize-winning porcelain faced children
           In the display cases.
I Feel You . . .
    Because
        You are always present in my thoughts
        My heart, My loneliness,
            My joy or disappointment.

Patricia Ann Woolfork

I keep waiting to hear you call my name
    When I enter a room or
        Walk through a doorway
            Filled with longing for your advice
            Your unconditional love
            Your friendship
            Your smiling, accepting face.

I can still feel the coolness and moisture of your hands
I can still hear the resonant melody within your laughter.

I Feel You . . .
    Now as I have always done and will continue
    Until my sight, sound and heartbeat
    Make escape into the universe of limitless possibility

        Will I Feel You . . .
            Even then?

REFLECTION OF A FRIENDSHIP— THE EULOGY

4:00 a.m.
My beautiful friend, LaVonne,
How will I live without you in my life?
You have been an integral part
Of it for over fifty years!
How will I go through a day, a week,
Without talking to you on the phone,
Making you laugh –
You, listening to my tears?
How will a memory not cause
A tear to slide down my face?

We just spent several hours, on the phone,
Laughing,
Joking,
Sharing milestones,
Speaking of grandchildren.
You called me your sister/friend –
More than friends –
SOUL Sisters!
We loved unconditionally,
With whole hearts,
Never holding back
Through the good times and the bad.

You were the most uplifting, positive,
Inspirational, tell me like it is person,
I have ever believed in and trusted implicitly.
The most caring, patient, compassionate,
Loving and loyal friend to anyone
Fortunate enough to get into her inner circle.

What a privilege to be her BEST FRIEND –
Besides her husband and kids, and

Grandchildren, of course, but,
I KNEW HER LONGER!
This is the greatest loss of my life.
We were Celie without Nettie and vice versa.
We had a special place in each other's heart.
We never ended a conversation
Without reaffirming our love.
How will I endure never
Hearing her voice or her laugh again?
How can I endure
Not having you to LOVE me?
You have been my constant,
Consistent,
Unconditional,
Soul companion!
MY HEART IS
RIPPING,
TORN,
MUCH MORE THAN BREAKING!

We have known each other since 3rd grade –
Best friends since 9th grade.
We'd go to school together,
Eat lunch together,
Have most classes together,
Ride the bus back home together, and
Still get on the phone for a couple of hours
Every single day!
You taught me how to sew, knit and crochet.
You taught me what friendship means.
Oh, how you would get me
About using the word "friend"
Too loosely, too prematurely!
Who will I trust
With my secrets and vulnerabilities?

I MISS YOU ALREADY!!!!!

I have cried every minute

Savoring Eden

Since I heard the news –
Ten hours and counting . . .
ALONE –
Without you to comfort me.
ALONE –
Unable to comfort our family back home.

In spite of my grief,
I am happy about a few things:
She had the best husband and
The most attentive and adoring children.
She got a chance to be
A doting and devoted grandmother.
She knew that she was loved and appreciated,
And she shared them and all that love with me.
My strength comes from the knowledge
That she truly loved us.

Who else will love Patches more than you?
How will Benji and Bella get comfortable at night
Without you as the pillow?
I am happy you got to enjoy being a grandmother.
I always said that I wanted to be one of your animals,
But that care and affection pales in comparison
To the attention that Angelica and Blake received!
Wasn't it GREAT?

I will think of you every time I see an elephant,
Wear something pink,
Remember your smile and your laughter.
I will not let you down my dear friend.
I will continue to make you proud of me.
Your love was not wasted on me!
Every piece of prose I write in the future
Will be dedicated to you
As was the first one in the book.
Every time I sit in this recliner and
Look at the room you said I made beautiful,
I will share a moment with you.

Patricia Ann Woolfork

I will imagine you talking to me
As the fire flickers in the fireplace, and
As the lights twinkle on the every season tree.

When I see a beautiful Alabama sky or sunset,
I will see it through your eyes and smile.
You sent me here to be in a better place
Even if it was without you –
Never a selfish bone in your body!

You deserve a bejeweled halo
And golden-tipped wings just because
You loved me in spite of myself.
Sometimes, more than I did.

Tell Butch "hello."
Mommy Peaches is waiting, and
Daddy Clarence remembers his little girl again!
Maybe Rasheema will sing to you
With her ever angelic voice.
Tell her I miss her too.
Bob and Dot are there, too.
Oooooo, don't forget Bernie!
Bet he still thinks he's fine.
Evelyn is probably grinning as I write these lines.

My friend, My mentor,
My cheerleader, My counselor,
My confidant,
My little sister – I had you by 19 days!
You knew me better than I know myself.

You know I got mad at HIM again!
I asked, "What lesson do I still need to learn?"
I didn't cuss HIM out this time.
I will wait on HIM . . . .
To provide me a safe place,
To provide all my needs,
To heal my physical and mental anguish

Savoring Eden

To make me more like you in
Gentility,
Gentleness,
Kindness, Patience,
Long-Suffering and
Loyalty.
I MISS YOU!!!!!!!!!!

Help me LORD,
To make it through this night and
Into dawn's early light!
Rest my precious.
Take a load off.
You ran a fine race.
We'll catch up soon.
Longevity is over-rated,
BUT YOU ARE GONE TOO SOON!
I will love you with every breath I will take
From this day forward until my last.

WE ALL MISS YOU!

I will do my best to comfort
ALL that we loved dearly.
My love and sympathy go to out to . . .
Leroy, Roy, Shara, Alexis, Mike, Angelica, Blake and
All the extended family that counted me as one of their own.

LORD,
Give us the strength needed to get through
This monumental change in our daily existence.
Let us continue to support each other in our sorrow,
And make our bond stronger.
Protect our hearts and health and
Send your Grace to protect us in our travel,
From near and far, to make tribute
To our most beloved LaVonne.

Rest darling girl.

Patricia Ann Woolfork

I am making my way to you.
I know HE will provide the way.
You can count on me to be there
For those you loved the most.
I will find the strength to be strong for them.
You know that, right?

Always your devoted sister/friend,
Patricia Ann Woolfork

                LaVonne Marie Adams-Hopkins
                    (9/29/49 – 11/25/14)

I MISS YOU GIRL!

Words cannot express how profoundly I am missing you.
Everyday a memory of our friendship stirs my tears and
Causes them to flow down my plump cheeks.
Whether good or bad – The response remains the same.

I remember . . . How badly I acted in secret
When you got the cancer diagnosis – How I cussed God
For trying to take You, my best and only friend,
Away from me.

I remember . . . Staying in my bed for two weeks
After each chemo treatment
Until it was time to take you for the next dose –
Always using a poker face of confidence and positivity
While seeing you, and sounding jovial while on the phone.
I remember . . .
Rejoicing over your beating that big, bad enemy!

I remember . . .
Our sushi, crabs, steak, and Jimmy Buff's, and
How you couldn't bring yourself to go to our favorite haunts
Without me.
I remember . . .
You telling me that I was your sister and
How much you loved me.

I remember . . . The surprise bridal shower you gave me,
The gifts you gave my daughter when her babies were born,
The treasure trove of baby clothes, furniture, etc.
You bestowed upon my son for my newest granddaughter.
I remember . . .
Your joy with the birth of your grandchildren, and
How we went crazy shopping for baby stuff.

Patricia Ann Woolfork

I remember . . . You listening to and encouraging me
About my poetry throughout the years.
I am writing this,
Unable to share it with you
Just like the other composed pieces written since you died.

I want to believe . . .
That you are looking over my shoulder
As I write, but
All I can see is . . .
You stretched out in that casket
With your hair still damp
As I coached the stylist
As how to fix your hair and makeup
Before the big day.

I pause now . . .
As the tears fall onto these pages and
Blurs the ink, and
My sobs grow louder, and my eyes burn.
I feel . . .
EMPTY
ALONE
ABANDONED.
How do I make this pain go away?

I am still using my poker face and voice
with your loved ones –
I am not fully certain if I am only a reminder
Of their awesome loss –
Wondering how soon the texts will stop and
The phone calls cease.
I haven't heard from your son or daughter-in-law
Since I came home after the funeral.
I only get reports of them through your husband.
When we talk, as promised,
a couple of times a week.

Savoring Eden

I wear some of your clothes that were given to me,
And feel guilty and depraved
Despite knowing you would want me to have them –
I would rather see you in them –
The two of us shopping and sharing a meal.

I had to remove your picture off my phone contact list
Because every time a call came in from your number,
I would jump up to talk to you and be reminded . . .
YOU ARE GONE!
Now your husband's face is in your place, and
It makes me smile when I see it
Because I know how much he loved us both.
My hope is that our talks are comforting
I am afraid that my façade will crack
And the deluge of my grief
Will be too painful for him to hear.

Now I talk with my therapist about you,
Or I talk to you with my pen.
I share them with him, and like you,
He gives me encouragement to keep writing.
He thinks I do it quite well just as you did.

So, I will continue to fight through the tears,
The ache in my chest, and the tightness in my throat
To open up my heart through my creative voice
So that the healing can begin.
I know that is what you would expect of me, but
I AM LOST WITHOUT YOU,

My dearest best sister/friend,
Watch over me if you can.
I grow tired of being the STRONG one!
The tears come less frequently,
but are easily triggered.
Never a day goes past without thinking about you.
I still go for the phone to tell you something, and

Patricia Ann Woolfork

It's been almost nine months since your passing.
I miss you every day, but
You are still here in my heart and in my thoughts.

I am almost jealous.
You don't have to put up with the barrage of BS
That we do every day. LOL
I miss you because . . .
I can't remember shit, and I can't ask you about it –
Like what's my password for QVC. LOL

Really, though,
There is a void I have been unable to fill, and
I don't think anyone can understand . . .
Except, maybe, my therapist. LOL
There is hope for me yet.
I must remember those words.

I am continuing to write my poetry.
If only, I could get the ball rolling for the publishing fees . . .
You have connections now, right?
Give your best sister/friend . . .
"The Hook Up" LOL
I MISS YOU GIRL!

MY FIRST XMAS WITHOUT YOU

Though this Xmas comes with its challenges
Because of the losses we have recently experienced,
We have our great memories
Of those we loved and who especially loved us
To keep us looking forward.

May our tears become joyful and
Let peace reside in our broken hearts once more.
They are preparing a place for us and
Will watch over us ….
UNTIL WE MEET AGAIN!

Love to everyone
Who is taking a walk in our shoes
This holiday season.*
Keep the spirit alive
Just as they
Would have wanted us to do.
Love to each and every one of you.
May we be blessed
With a happier New Year in 2015!

*Dedicated to the Hopkins/Adams/Portee family,
Tracey Parker, Jim Simms, and my Facebook Friends*

Patricia Ann Woolfork

A Tribute in So Many Words

Loyal, loving, leader, legendary, logical, love, laughter, lover
Optimistic, opinionated, open-minded, over-protective,
Unique, unassuming, unswerving, unbelievable, unpretentious,
Intelligent inspiring, industrious, inviting, icing on the cake
Strong, stern, sentimental, spontaneous, simple, solid, steady,

Jovial, joyful, judicious, juvenile
Over-the-top, outstanding, obdurate, original, observant
Humorous, honest, hovering, heroic, hilarious, handsome, hunk
Notable, nutty, notoriously funny
Supportive, sympathetic, sociable, studious, scary, sexy
Outrageously witty, outlandish
Nice, neighborly, nurturing

Affectionate, awesome, adventurous, active (duty), astonishing,
Devoted, delightful, determined, direct, darling, down-to-earth, dynamic, dashing,   diligent, dancer, debonair, Dad
Amazing, admired, adored, adoring, apple of Mom's eye
Military, masculine, motivated, mentor, musical, money maker, movie buff
Sensible, superhero, silly, smart, secretive shopper, stubborn

August 14, 1942 – June 14, 2015

These were the words I asked family and friends to give me to best describe this wonderful man, and I used them to spell out his name

Eulogy for Louis Johnson Adams

Louis Adams was my best friend LaVonne's older brother. The first memory of my having a crush on him was when I saw his picture in his Air Force uniform in their living room. That was somewhere between 9 to 14 years old. He was soooooooooo fine! I'd only seen him in person probably once in the 57-year friendship I had with his sister.

It was not until LaVonne's death two days before Thanksgiving last year that I finally got to see him again at her funeral. I walked over to him and introduced myself to him and Jacque—confessed my childhood crush to them both—and proceeded to tell him that he was still pretty fine!

I was blessed with the privilege of eulogizing my sister/friend LaVonne—the hardest thing I have ever done! But it was Louis and Jacque that chose to sit next to me during the service, and when I returned to my seat, it was Louis who put his arm around me and let me rest my head on his shoulder as I rocked back and forth trying to hold back the scream trying to escape my lips as the tears streamed down my face.

From that fateful day, December 5, 2015, Louis and Jacque claimed me. Jacque would send encouraging texts and call me and after we talked, I would talk to Louis, and he would tell me that they loved me and would be there for me because of the bond LaVonne and I shared.

They knew how profoundly traumatic her loss was for me. It was because of the connection we made on that fateful day, that although brief in its endurance, our friendship was solid between the three of us, and our conversations ended just as they always did with LaVonne, "I Love You."

So I am here today to say good-bye to my brother/friend, Louis, through my poetry and my words just as my sister/friend, LaVonne, would have wanted in her absence and to support my new sister/friend, Jacque. In fact, Jacque insisted on it. She said that Louis would want me here to share this moment with all of us who loved him.

Although we are saddened by this loss, we can gather strength and comfort in the knowledge that Louis is no longer in pain. He went the way he wanted—at home with his family. Now he is back in the loving arms of his mom and dad and the little sister he adored. What a party they must be having together! They will watch over us "Until We Meet Again."

June 23, 2015
(August 14, 1942 – June 14, 2015)

June 26, 2015
Monument, Colorado

Even in the midst of natural beauty,
ugliness can rear its evil head.
However, I will not succumb
to my human tendency to surrender.
I will keep my peace,
enjoy the tranquility around me,
bathe in the presence of God,
and allow Him to direct all of my steps.

Dear Lord:
Use me as your vessel
to comfort, encourage, and
show love, affection and tolerance
to my dear friend in this time of grief
and life-changing circumstances.
Help me not to take things personally,
to be more empathetic and sympathetic,
but remain true to myself and my spiritual preservation.
I must remember that I, too,
have not fully completed the steps of grieving and
that this death
has reopened fresh wounds with my own loss.
I must maintain my compassion
so that we both come out on the other side in victory.

Only YOU Lord can make this miracle happen.
Your Grace and Loving Kindness will prevail
and be the covering and safety net needed
during these troubling times.
Let us be a comfort and not a burden to each other.
Let us speak truth to each other
and mourn our losses together in sisterly love
as both of our loved ones would want us to do.

Patricia Ann Woolfork

I thank you Lord
for these blessings you have already bestowed on us
and for the opportunity
to show our gratefulness for your faithfulness.
This is my solemn desire –
to please You Lord and to be your faithful servant.
Forgive me for my short comings,
my arrogance, anger, and stubbornness,

Help me Lord
to become more conscious
of my role in controlling my diabetes and other ailments.
HEAL me Lord
so that I can better honor you
and be a testimony of Your Divinity.

July 1, 2015
Monument, Colorado

Today has been a rough day.
I woke up trying to figure out
what year LaVonne and I met.
Was it third grade or fourth?
I immediately thought I
should call her to get clarification,
and then I remembered. . .

She died nearly eight months ago.
In the darkness of my bedroom, I
could feel the tears roll from my eyes
as I remembered
that I could never call her again
to ask her to remind me
about anything, ever, again.
The sense of loss is unbearable once again,
and the tears are cascading
down my freckled cheeks
onto my chin and onto the top of my dress.

I am sitting outside on the front porch
of her devoted brother, Louis' house, who has also died.
His memorial service was just a week ago yesterday.
I am here in Monument, Colorado to
comfort his wife and my new friend, Jacque,
for her tremendous loss.
We are together to comfort each other,
make sure business matters are taken care of
and to just share our grieving together.

I am not sure what can make the pain
in your heart grow fainter, less tight, and weighty.
I only wish it would go somewhere else
as I feel the tightening in my jaw and travel down my neck.
I try to concentrate on the sounds around me –

Patricia Ann Woolfork

the whistle of a bird – the buzzing of a fly –
the gentle ting of the wind chime –
the rush of wind
as it meanders up the winding road and
makes the branches
of the pine trees in the front yard sway
and resettle themselves.
I hear a chirp I haven't heard before.
It's coming from my right,
the caw of a crow from my left.

I wonder if
Louis and LaVonne are somewhere
shaking their heads at my foolish emotional display.
Shouldn't I rather be rejoicing because
they are no longer suffering from pain and disease?
Of course, I am,
BUT their memories,
or the lack of making new ones together,
are so utterly painful.
I am unable to keep the tears inside my head!

I am surrounded by beauty
in a place once filled with lots of love and laughter,
but my selfish side only wants what's been lost.
I want her back!
And then,
I wonder. . .
If I had gone first,
would LaVonne be reacting the same as I am?
Would she be struggling
with finding peace,
the anger of loss, the extreme loneliness, and
the heartbreak of life without me in it?

We were supposed to be two little old ladies
sitting on a bench trying to remember the good ole' days,
listening to the laughter
of our grand and great-grandchildren

as they play and give us hugs and kisses.

How will Leroy and Jacque
get over not seeing their faces,
holding their hands,
kissing their lips,
sharing a bed and
all the other pleasant and mundane daily things
they did together?
I don't know what losing a mate is like.
Mine either walked out or got tossed out –
nothing long-term like forty-six and
twenty-nine years of marriage.

The only comparison I have
is my relationship with my best friend –
talking, crying, hugging,
cooking, sewing, knitting,
shopping, eating, travelling,
celebrating, etc., etc.
We shared secrets, sickness, deaths, weddings, births.
We had weekly rituals of shopping and eating out.
We talked nearly every day.
I'd call to read her
everything I'd write on my prosaic journey.
She'd even come to my performances of
"An Evening of Poetry and Jazz with Trishann & Friends."
She was my cheerleader,
my mentor,
my guidance counselor,
my shrink,
my sister,
my best, best friend.

I MISS YOU!
My tears are staining these pages I write upon today.
The gentle wind slowly dries the tears on my face,
and the sun begins to creep onto the porch where I sit.
I am reminded that I have been left in good hands.

Patricia Ann Woolfork

HE will continue to restore my soul, heal my heart,
open new doors to bring new people into my life,
perhaps another will love me as much as you did,
and as much as I loved and still love you.

I will try to remember . . . that you are in the breeze,
the call of the birds, the sights and sounds all around me.
This is your presence, your out-pouring of love.

I will look for you in nature and talk to you with my pen.
You can read over my shoulder and
whisper with a memory
to keep me knowing?
I was once loved unconditionally –
and keep that knowledge alive in my heart.
And as for you, Louis Johnson Adams,
I will always remember your kindness and acceptance
and ever so brief friendship
as well as that sexy smile and laughter.
You are also gone too soon, but
you and LaVonne
and your mom and dad have much catching up to do.
Our spirits will meet up again.
I will see you again someday
and tell you how "fine" you are.

In the meantime, you all watch over us down here
who miss you and love you.
Protect us and continue to guide us.
Isn't that what angels are supposed to do
Enough said. XOXOXOXO

I Talk to You with Pen in Hand

I miss you.
You would have been right here in the thick of things
Unpacking
Sorting
Making choices
Repacking
Putting things into garbage bags.
Yet here I am, again,
Amid masses of confusion
Not at all like I left my things nearly four years ago –
Tossed around the rooms like trash
No respect for the contents,
The memories,
The years of sacrifice to obtain them –
Church hats crushed beneath heavy objects
Boxes marked "fragile" tossed
Like pizza dough against furniture.

I miss you.
You would have given me encouraging words
You would have told me not to fret –
We'd get through this –
Together.

You would not have kept me guessing
If it was being moved back with me or stored somewhere.
You would have loaned me what I needed
Without hesitation and certainly
Without reneging on your promise to do so.

Now here I am to face the disappointment and bewilderment
Without you –
My compass
My voice of reason
Without you – Telling me not to be discouraged.
I miss you.

You are not here to cheer me on through the pain in my body
Caused by the lifting and moving of both cardboard and
Plastic boxes of dirty clothes and trash not mine
Just to be able to get into corners over piles
To find my precious belongings.

I miss you.
You are not here to dry my tears of dejection and outrage
Over how callously my home has been abused
By those I trusted to hold down the fort.

I feel as though my house has been vandalized and
Squatted upon by vagrants –
Like my pants had been pulled down, and
I have been ceremoniously raped from one room to the next
As I survey the damage done either by neglect or
Lack of heat –
Cracked plaster –
Missing parts of sheetrock on the ceiling –
Brand new door sawn through by firemen because
An extension cord going from one landing to the next
Had started a fire because
The utility bill had not been paid and
The deadbolt was locked from the inside because
Someone panicked and exited through a back door.

Weeping over . . .
Filthy carpet
Carpet cut from the hallway
Exposing the wood floor beneath
Like another bested enemy –
Dirt and dust
Grease caked stove
Mouse droppings
Pictures hanging askew
Family pictures and important keepsakes –
Ravaged by dripping water and mold.
There is no heat or water
In this place I used to call home.

Savoring Eden

Plastic bags line the toilet filled with paper towels.
I must use this as my comfort station
When my bladder cannot hold out any longer, and
I wait to get back to the civilized world at your house.

I miss you because . . .
Although I cuss and scream,
You are not here to tell me "STOP!"
"Take a breath."
"No one will treat your things like you –
Not even your child."

I miss you because . . .
Talking to you
Without hearing a response from your lips,
Only makes me miss you more –
Makes me feel alone in the world again –
Makes me the lone warrior
Without advisors and strategists
To plan the next attack of "Find and Seek"
Remember to look for . . .

I am sure I will get through this
Like ever so many challenges before, but
I can't help missing you.

FRIENDSHIP

A gentle push in the right direction,
A pat on the back for a deed well done,
A telephone call to say, "Hello,"
A card for no occasion at all,
A flower to bring good cheer,
A smile for success,
A tear shed in gladness,
An embrace shared in sorrow,
A secret kept,
A promise unbroken,
Loyalty,
Trust,
Faith without question –
Such is the essence of Friendship.

Written to my best friend, LaVonne Marie Adams-Hopkins, 1970

THE FIRST ANNIVERSARY, NOVEMBER 25, 2015

I am not sure if I can articulate the numerous emotions
That are propelling me through this day.
Today marks the 1st Anniversary of the death of my best friend.
It is hard to believe that a whole year has gone by, but
On the other hand, not so unbelievable.
I spent so much of it suspended in the other world of
Seemingly never-ending grief.

It is difficult to explain to most people
What it means to have a best friend
Better still, what it means to be one.
It is such a rarity today
What with all the social media and electronic devices
That further impede our ability to make the time
To make a phone call, write a handwritten letter, or
Send a meaningful card,
Meet for lunch,
Go shopping in thrift stores and farmers' markets,
Make reservations to share Thanksgiving together;
But that is what real best friends do.

For 51 out of 57 years that is what we did.
Our phone calls would last for hours
As we'd multi-task on speakerphone.
There wasn't a single thing she didn't know about me, and
She loved me anyway!

I would be lying if I told you that I have my act together.
The simplest memory evokes both laughter and tears.
The urge to pick up the phone and tell her something comical
Still catches me off guard.
In that infinitesimal instant –
I forget – Plunging me head first – Into my new state of reality.
You see, there is no one
I can expose my degree of loss to because

Patricia Ann Woolfork

I have to be the ever-strong one for everyone else, but
That is my role, and I wholeheartedly accept it.

It sucks to be an only child and lose your best sister/friend.
She is probably shaking her head and
Willing me to shut up, but
She knows the real me inside and out . . .
She knows that my words are my healing and
That I simply must share them from time to time.

My lashes are clogged by my tears.
My tears are not all sad tears.
I also cry in appreciation of the wonderful gift God loaned me
All those years ago.
He allowed us time to see our children grow into adults,
Get married, and become parents themselves.
He allowed us time with our grandchildren as a "do-over"
For the things we didn't do quite right and to shower them
With more love than we thought we had in us.

I am blessed because she did not linger in pain
As we looked on helplessly.
I am blessed because I got to tell her about
Her diamond encrusted halo and gold-tipped wings
Waiting for her because she was my best sister/friend –
A name she gave me.
I am blessed because
I heard her tell me that she loved me one last time
Just hours before she went home to be with our Lord.
My God is Great and full of Mercy and Grace.
He is my Rock and will see me through any storm –
Just like this one.

GRIEF REVISITED:
I AM A WORK IN PROGRESS

I have made some strides in my journey through grief.
I am more accepting of both my strengths and weakness.
I am making strives to improve on them.
The light is shining upon my self-love.
I am owning my own mess.

I am more socially and spiritually active.
I am still writing and prepping my manuscript.
I am making myself emotionally open to new people.
I am sharing my story with others
Who have childhood traumas and
Helping them in their healing and
Gleaning from the rewards of doing so.

The feeling I get is indescribable
When someone responds and trusts me to tell me theirs.
I provide them with a fresh outlook because of my maturity.
It gives my life purpose
Outside of my own goals and desires.

I look forward to facing this New Year
With gusto and determination, and
To make it my best year yet,
In this, the beginning of my 66th year.

It is all about me, finally!
I have seen too many leave too soon.
I have things yet to check off my list, and
Only I can prevent them from coming to fruition.

Patricia Ann Woolfork

I pray for our health and safety.
I pray for us to accomplish all of our goals.
I pray that we let God direct, not only our steps, but
Those who are about to lead us.
We must place our burdens in His hands,
And leave them there.

I pray that our loved one not be gunned down in the streets.
I pray that God's Will be done in all things.
I pray that His Grace and Mercy supply all of our needs.
I pray that He obliterates all bigotry and hatred from our hearts.
I pray that we become
Manifestations of
His Love for us here on earth!
Can I get an Amen?

DEAR RASHEEMA,

I have been thinking about you these last few days, and I thought it necessary to write you this letter in order to thank you for all the things you have done for me over these many years.

I want you to know that even though I don't often tell you or show you that I care about you, because of the turmoil my own life is in, I think you have some very special qualities, you are loved, and you are appreciated!

I'm sorry that you have felt neglected. It wasn't my intention to do so. I'm sorry I don't come downstairs on a regular basis. It's just that some time, I don't even want to face myself let alone someone else. It's like I'm in my cocoon inside my bedroom, and lately I'm only coming out to go to church or some other church function or the dentist. That certainly is no way to conduct a life. I am working on improving myself.

I wish I could have been more like you. You have loads of friends. You have a magnificent talent. You've traveled all over the world. You have good credit. You've kept your beauty and your youth. You have freedom to do what you please when you please. You are not accountable for anyone other than yourself.

I am also proud of you for going back to school. I really admire you for that. In so many ways, I want to be like you when I grow up! (Smile)

Please accept my sincere apologies if I have hurt you in any way during these last several months. You are important to me on so many levels. I haven't forgotten that you have called me your daughter. I love you. I hope you can love me just as I am and as I hope to be.

Always, *Patricia Ann*
Rasheema passed away 11/12/14 after a bout with Dementia

Patricia Ann Woolfork

Dear Stella,

It is with much sadness that I extend my condolences to you and your daughters for the loss of your beloved husband and father. It is my hope that the poem that I have written for such an occasion as this brings you comfort and peace of mind.

People may say they know what you are going through. However well their intentions are, no one knows how you feel, or how this loss will affect you. Rest assured that Our Heavenly Father does know and will keep you throughout this new journey in which you find yourselves. God makes no promises that He cannot keep. His Word says that there will come a time when there will be no more death, disease, or pain, and that He will wipe away all of our tears. (Revelations 21: 3, 4)

Stella, it was so good hearing your voice again this morning after so many years. Please call on me whenever you need someone to talk to—my ears and my heart are open for you, my friend. I will never forget how tenderly you cared for me these many years ago. Let me try to do the same for you now.

I look forward to spending time with you in the near future so that we can play catch up for all the lost time.

With much love and affection,

September 18, 2009

UNTIL WE MEET AGAIN

How many times did I want to call,
Come by and visit
Yet found ever so many excuses?
Too busy?
Too tired?
So overwhelmed was I with sorrow and guilt.
I was unhappy because
My best friend lay hopelessly dying.
I was filled with grief and guilt that it was not me instead.

I remember our good times.
I remember your zest and vigor for life.
How pained was I seeing you lying in that hospital bed –
Crazed with the fact that I could neither help nor heal.
Remembering the you that was –
Smacked in the face –
With the reality of the you
You had become.

If only we could turn back time and
Erase the myriad of mistakes made,
Relate all of the unsaid, "I love you(s)",
Make up for all the time lost,
Accept responsibility,
Admit vulnerability,
Apologize just because.

You were my friend.
I will always remember you and forever miss you.
You came. You saw. You made your mistakes.
You paid the price, and you have conquered this life.

Patricia Ann Woolfork

My hope is that you have now gone to a higher plain
Where disease and pain no longer have a hold on you,
That you can gaze upon those of us left behind
That loved you, and know
That you are truly missed.

Please watch over and protect us from ourselves.
Thank you for your many years of friendship.
Remembering them will sustain me . . .
UNTIL WE MEET AGAIN

*Dedicated to the late Jay S.T. Garrett (1/ 29/1994) and
the friends and families of others who have suffered through the
AIDS pandemic.*

MY BLEEDING HEART

How do I to tell you how much I miss you?
My heart bleeds every birthday, holiday,
Special event, and especially Mother's Day.
You are in my thoughts – always in my heart –
Always in my prayers.

What wrong could I have done
To make you abandon the entire family
Twenty years have passed since I last saw your face.
Your words still haunt me:
"I am not ready to have a relationship with the family."

Am I a grandmother, how many times, boys or girls?
You are an uncle to eight children –
That baby nephew, who was in the shopping cart,
Is now in college and just turned twenty-one.
Your first nephew is twenty-five and married.
His mom is married with another son and daughter.
Your sister has another son and a daughter.
Your brother has another son and three daughters.

My father is dead and your grandmother has dementia.
My best friend, LaVonne, has died.
Your father lost his third wife a year ago.
Your Aunt Margie has passed away.
Your brother is living at your grandparent's house.
Your sister and I are living in Huntsville, Alabama.

I know that there are some things
For which I need to ask for your forgiveness.
I wasn't perfect – no parent is, but
There were extenuating circumstances, and
You never let me explain.
What I have found out . . .

Patricia Ann Woolfork

Your aunt had told you a lie, and thankfully,
She is dead now, too,
I hope she rots in hell, if there is one.
You believed her lies without ever talking to me, and
We all lost you and your love.

What happened to my "Yacky Clacky"?
You used to be my shadow.
I never had to worry about your being okay.
I was always proud of you.
I loved you so much, and that has not changed.
My heart mourns your loss in my life.
It has not been the same since those words were spoken.

I really miss my little blue-eyed baby.
Your sister has a son with those blue eyes.
He acts so much like you.
I often call him by your name.
He doesn't like to eat meat just like you.
He is also very fair skinned just like you, and
He is very smart, too.

I have tried to find you.
I found a phone number once, left a message, but
I never heard from anyone.
I hope I can rest my eyes upon your sweet face
Before I take my last breath.
My heart bleeds for you my darling boy.
My prayers continue to go forth
For your good health, happiness and prosperity.
I will always love you
And There Is Nothing You Can Do About It!

Dedicated to my son, Vaughann Christian Simmons DOB 8/26/72 – gone since 1995

LOSS COMES IN ALL FORMS

I've had several months to try to digest what happened to a six-year friendship. I cannot say that I have really settled on any one factor, but I can tell you that it has left me crushed to my core. You broke me.

What are you supposed to do when you have done everything in your power to be the best friend and companion to someone that you felt was an extension of your family—someone you would defend to the death to make sure no harm would come to them—someone you would slip and call "mom" because that was the type of devotion you had to that person.

What happens when strangers to you, but family to them, come in to destroy a perfectly good relationship with innuendo and false accusations and character assassination? How am I to feel when I was not even defended, the truth told about my character, or our relationship fought for after six years without any incident or argument between us?

This is someone I took to the doctor, made sure their blood pressure was okay, monitored their blood sugar, went grocery shopping for, found medical equipment to make their independence even easier—not to mention the hours spent talking about the good old days—learning about my new city—making food and sharing meals with at least once a week—if you saw me, you saw her.

Now here I am without my friend, with neighbors becoming more distant without even knowing the facts, and me feeling abandoned yet again by someone who knew nearly everything about my past history with my parents and spouses.

When I finally found out what I had been accused of on social media, I was dumbstruck. When I attempted to defend myself, even my faith was challenged. Even those that knew me better than that, whose weight I helped them bare in caring for their family member, did not even challenge the accusations nor talk to me about them, tore my heart.

But like I said in my response: the truth will outweigh the lies. God has a way of closing doors in order to open new ones. He allows people into your life for periods of time to help you get to the next level and to make you stronger and wiser, less trusting and more self-protecting.

I will never allow someone else to move me to become someone that I am not. I am "what you see is what you get": friendly, unselfish, caring, empathetic, and genuine, and sensitive. I may not be the typical person you are accustomed to because I come at a situation from my heart. When I offer my friendship, it is without conditions—I believe you to be just like me in that regard until proven otherwise.

This betrayal has been the most painful event in my life since the death of my best friend, LaVonne Marie Adams-Hopkins, four years ago. Yet another thing I had to go through without her to talk me through it, comfort me, and push me to get over it. Thankfully, Dr. Sandy is still with me to counsel me and advise me. He believes in my honor and integrity and realizes how it has stirred up my "abandonment" issues, and he challenges me to not give up on people—to continue to offer my friendship. But, like LaVonne used to warn me, "Don't throw the word 'friend' around too quickly or loosely. Everyone does not deserve that title. It is a treasure. It has to be earned."

So my dear girl, I am still listening to your counsel. I feel your love even though I miss you most profoundly. I am still a work in progress, but you should be proud of me. I am finally getting this book published!

And as for my former "friend," I am sorry that our relationship did not mean as much to you as it did for me. I regret that you chose to cast me aside rather than fight to keep me in your life. I miss you. I have been advised to stay away from you because your family may cause me grief because they think they might lose something they want from you because of your love for me. I do believe in my heart that you loved me. I believe you were intimidated by your late husband's children and you felt you had to choose them over me even though I have never laid eyes on them in the six years that I have known you.

I choose to forgive you. I am hurt to my core, nevertheless. We both lost something special and beautiful and very dear to me. I am, however, grateful for the time we had. You are a very remarkable lady. I still cry at the thought of losing you because of your ninety-five years, but who knows, you may outlive me at the rate I am going. I have got to let go of stress and heartbreak before it does me in. Shucks, I got way too much left to do past my sixty-nine years.

Good-bye

Death of a friendship. May 16, 2012 – April 28, 2018

FIELD OF DREAMS

Your winning smile flashed through my thoughts tonight.
Even though you are no longer here to converse with me,
I hear your voice.
I know your message now
And only regret I could not thank you
Before you departed on your journey
I know now how much you truly cared and believed in me.
I miss you all the more
For being the real friend I was unable to fully recognize.
How lucky we were to share our few moments.
You found your field of dreams,
And bequeathed a plot to me
Upon which to nurture my own.
Thank you.

Dedicated to the late Zarfa Locadia, Esq. 1953-1989

Dearest Susan,

If someone says, "I know how you feel," they mean well. Unless you have lost a mother or your best friend, you don't know! If you lost your best friend, then I can tell you, I know how you feel.

I know that Jo was also your best friend, so I can relate to that type of loss. The difference between us is that you have siblings to help carry the burden of grief.

You will feel it most when you go to pick up the phone to tell her something you forgot to tell her, or when you look for her to come through the front doors at Mayfair Towers to start her exercise for the day.

You do, however, have the multitude of memories that will forever bring both a tear and a twinkle in your eyes when you take that moment to smile.

There must be an awesome reunion up there in heaven with hugging and kissing, singing and dancing. Your mother is with your handsome and adoring daddy. She did not have to wait too long to see her two best friends, your auntie and her Texas partner. They are probably line dancing as we speak. Maybe she'll run across Elinor and Rena, Chucky Baby and Linda. The possibilities are limitless.

I know she didn't want to leave her babies, but it was her time to go. She fought a long, hard fight, but she really missed her husband. I bet they are holding hands right now and looking down at their legacy left behind. They did a great job with the values they instilled in you all. I am truly impressed with how you turned out. You are a jewel!

I will miss seeing her stroll in with her perfectly coiffed hair, polished nails, and her bling. She sparkled from her hair to her toes. She had spunk. She was kind and giving. I am so sorry that she never got to show me how to use my KitchenAid Stand Mixer,

Patricia Ann Woolfork

but I am grateful for the recipes she shared with me. She will be missed as a person and a presence.

I want to thank you from the bottom of my heart for these six years of sharing your mother with me. I will always remember breaking bread with your family at home, at church, at Lawler's, and at Mayfair Towers. Please extend my deepest condolences to your brothers and sister, your nieces and nephews, your sons, and your granddaughters.

My heart is breaking for you. I don't know of a more life altering experience than losing your very best friend also embodied in a parent.

I am here for you if you need an ear, a shoulder, a hug, or a companion. I did not have that when LaVonne died. It may have helped. So I extend that invitation to you, in all sincerity. You have been awesome to me. I would like to return the favor. If there is anything you need, simply ask.

I am so deeply sorry for your loss. I will continue to pray for you and your family as I have done each week since I found out about your Mom's health. God is in control, and He will not give us anything that we cannot bear—in His time.

I want to thank you for accepting me and welcoming me here at Mayfair Towers, and for taking such good care of us above and beyond—from your heart.

    Always,

Dedicated to "Jo" Virginia Tipton
(July 21, 1936 - July 15, 2018)
And Susan Hefley

FOR THOSE LEFT BEHIND

Weep not for me out of sadness.
My battle has been won.
Rejoice!
I am at peace.
I have found harmony in the universe.

I will miss . . . our intimate conversations, but
I will talk with you from time to time.
You will hear me –
At sunrise as the birds begin to sing
As I whisper in the raindrops.
As you read my words upon a page.
I will miss . . . seeing you face-to-face
Across the dinner table
When you awaken in the morning, but,
You will see me again –
In the beauty of a sunset,
A snow covered meadow,
A child's smile.
I will miss . . . holding your hand,
Kissing your face, but
I will touch you again –
With a memory,
Kiss you with the wind,
Embrace you with sunshine.

Weep not for me out of sadness.
Remember me always with gladness.
When you need a laugh, (my cheese-eating grin)*
Remember the silly things I'd say or do.
Remember me . . .
By fulfilling your own dreams,
Living your life to the utmost;
And most of all –
Remember. . . I Love You.
          Eugene Bernard Boykin, Jr. 12/9/91

An Adult Journey of Discovery

AN ADULT JOURNEY OF DISCOVERY

We all have the desire to express ourselves in various situations in order to get a point across, express an opinion, or communicate our various emotions.

Remember when we had that special song that we played when there was wine and candlelight? Let me take you there again. Or, how about when we were looking for a special card to show our significant other how much we thought about them? Enjoy the journey and take a flashback in time.

Believe it or not, the Hot and Spicy section was the most requested by fans at my performances at "An Evening of Poetry and Jazz with Trishann & Friends," unless minors were present. I do not believe them to be vulgar, simply sensuous. In fact, I have been dubbed the "sensuous poet with the melodious voice" when describing all facets of the human experience and our commune with each other and nature.

This portion "Love and Romance/Passion: Hot & Spicy," is the fun side of our life experiences. Yes, there are ups and downs when dealing with others, but when it's good—it's really good—for as long as it lasts.

Love and Romance

TO KNOW YOU IS TO . . .

You have been in my waking thoughts
And in my dreams at night.
I no longer feel alone
And for this I am thankful.

You've brought smiles to my lips
When others have failed.
The only tears in my eyes
Have been caused by laughter.

You are
Shining stars,
Sunshine and flowers.

You bring me joy, and
The security of knowing that
My future will be brighter
Having known you.

Dedicated to the late Edward "Butch" Caston

I WANT

I want to be needed.
I want to be appreciated.
I want to be held in the middle of the night.
I want to be loved passionately and completely.
I want to laugh at life's ups and downs,
Cry when I am happiest.
I want to be respected.
I want to be trusted
With the deepest secrets of your being.
I want to know every inch of you.

I want to go on expedition for life's true meaning.
I want to tremble at a touch, melt with a kiss.
I want to be missed when I am out of sight, but
Never out of mind.
I want to put the past behind me.
I want to bask in the sunshine
Of a happier today and a golden tomorrow.

I want to walk along the beach holding hands.
I want to stare at the waves,
Mesmerized . . . .
By the ebb and flow of a love for life
I have never before experienced.
I want to watch a sunrise with you next to me.
Embrace you tenderly at sunset.
I want to be as close to perfection
As any person can be for another.

I want to share your ups and downs,
Your joys and disappointments.
I want to cheer you on in the face of victory,
Listen when you need an ear,
Understand when you get confused.
I want to drink champagne by candlelight,
I want to get snowed in in a mountain cabin –

Savoring Eden

Bear skin rug, fireplace, and you beside me.
I want to make you laugh –
Make you cry with the joy of knowing me.

I want to be remembered at my death
As someone who made a difference.
I want my essence to touch many souls,
My words to bring comfort,
My tears – a lesson learned.

I want peace.
Peace of mind –
Peace of heart –
Peace of spirit – a piece of the good life.
I want to know that someone cares.
I want to bring a twinkle to your eyes,
A smile to your perfect lips.

I want to grow wiser with each passing day.
Make each moment count.
Waste not one precious second
Of a slowly . . .
Dwindling mortality.

I want it all –
With no reservations,
No remorse,
No guilt.
I want to share these experiences
With someone special –
Is it you?

I Keep Holding Back

I keep holding back from letting you know
How wonderful you make me feel,
Or rather, shall I say
How wonderful I feel when I am with you?
I keep holding back from letting you know
How much you mean to me.
I keep holding back from saying
How much I long for you when we are apart.
I keep holding back because
I don't want to SCARE you with my intensity!
I keep holding back,
Not because I am afraid or unsure.
I keep holding back because
I can't discern
If you are ready, willing, or able
To accept all that I have to give to you.

I keep holding back from shedding tears of joy
Each time we make love.
I keep holding back,
Teeth clenched against my tongue,
Trying not to utter the words, "I love you",
I am so afraid that my secret will be out,
But more afraid that you may not love me in return.

I keep holding back because
My honesty has undermined my track record for success.
I keep holding back because
I'm still holding on to the dream –
Scared to sleep – scared to be awake.
Do I trust myself?
Do I trust my intuition?
Do I trust my instinct? I've been so wrong before!

I can't bear the thought of losing you.
Oh, don't get me wrong!

Savoring Eden

I would survive,
But I, too, have been to the mountaintop
And the view is sweet.
You and me growing old together
Sharing time and space throughout eternity,
Soul mates finally found.

I keep holding back because
I've been afraid to live –
Afraid to demand my share of happiness.
Do I continue to make the same mistakes?
Can you read my mind?
I think not.
If you could, you'd already know
That I'm well on my way
To being completely and passionately in love with you.

I keep holding back,
But life has already passed me by.
What's left of life is too short, too precious.
Would you like to share part of what's left with me?
I keep holding back our future together.
Stop me if you can!

FIRST KISS

So, you say you've wondered
How will my lips feel against yours?
Do I dare tell you
That thought has also crossed my mind?
I feel like that school girl
About to get her first kiss –
Anxious
Yet cautious
Excited
Yet reserved
Gentle, innocent and endearing
The first kiss between us.

Now I am the one wondering
How will your arms feel around me?
Will I melt when
I look deeply into your warm, brown eyes?
Will our kiss be a feather's touch
Of lip against lip?
Will it be the spark igniting
The smoldering flame within us?

Our first kiss... Will it be the beginning or
The end of life as we know it?
There is only one way for us to find out.
Are you willing, as I am,
To let go of the past,
Look forward to a future
As friends and then lovers?
Will our first kiss be the first of many?
I am wondering about that.
Has that thought also crossed your mind?
Only time will tell.

STORYBOOK ROMANCE

I want a storybook romance.
I want the hearts and flowers,
The sunset walks,
The embrace under the moonlit sky,
The early morning kiss,
The late-night phone call,
The stroll along the beach arm in arm,
The greeting cards that say,
"I miss you", "I love you",
"You're the best that's ever happened to me."

I want the bells, the whistles, the fireworks,
The insatiable love-making,
The passionate kiss.
I want to smell your cologne on my pillow,
I want the candlelight bubble bath and
The morning shower for two.
I want to hear the words, "I love you"
And know that they are genuinely felt.

I want the hug just because.
I want the affectionate tap on the bottom,
The soft romantic music and
The snuggling by the fireplace.
I want to wear your shirt
Because the scent of you lingers there.
I want the stroll in the mall holding hands,
The knowing glances between us,
The silent messages of love we share.
I want a storybook romance –
A happy ever-after love for the two of us.

My Knight in Shining Armor

You're my knight in shining armor.
You are so strong, forceful, yet kind.
You've come to slay these dragons
That blow fire upon my dreams.

I feel the tensions fade
Each time I hear your voice.
I feel my heartbeat steady
When we embrace.
I am moved by your trust in me,
Inspired by your determination,
Mesmerized by your charm,
I am overwhelmed by your manliness.

You continue to show me
Tenderness, compassion and love.
Even though
Not much time has passed between us,
I know
I can love you despite my insecurities.

I feel blessed because
You have entered into my life.
I am no longer a damsel in distress, but
You are still my knight in shining armor.
We can now live together
In a kingdom of our own.

TRANSFORMATION

I watch you sleeping so peacefully,
Little boy in repose.
Your sudden innocence is so endearing.
The worries of adulthood no longer line your brow.
I want to touch your curls, and kiss your cheek.
You just bring out the best in me.

LOVE NEVER FAILS

God has led me to you
From this course I'll not stray
My life has changed completely
From what it was yesterday.
You are the one I've prayed for
Of this I have no doubt
My love keeps growing steadily,
My fire has not gone out.
You are my everything –
My pride,
My love,
My life.
I wish to be yours forevermore,
Your friend,
Your lover,
Your wife.

A Wedding Day Tribute Revisited

Today is your day, celebrate!
Remember what led you here.
Remain true to yourselves and each other.
Simple gestures are the most meaningful.
Cards and flowers usually work for her,
But jewelry's good too!

Remember to say, "I love you."
Remember that actions speak louder than words.
Let laughter soothe your souls.
Be happy.
Be healthy.
Be passionate.
Learn from your mistakes and forgive generously.
Treat each day as though it may be your last.
Have no regrets.

Remember the joy you are experiencing this day.
Remember this moment.
Remember that first kiss.
Remember the promises you made
Before God and this company.
Remember to trust, to hope, to endure.
Remember you are not alone and that you are loved.
These memories will sustain you.

Dedicated to Sharalynn & Michael 10/14/2006

Patricia Ann Woolfork

A WEDDING DAY TRIBUTE: A MOTHER'S WISH

Today is a day to remember with gladness and reverence
For you begin a new journey of discovery –
Your soul mate finally found.
You are bonded by faith, trust, hope,
Abiding love, and an enduring friendship.
Remember what led you to this course
And remain true to yourselves.
Remember to share, to care, to empathize,
To do unto each other as you want to have done to you.
Remember that you have entered into a partnership.
All opinions are valid.
Compromise is an essential ingredient to success.
Remember that simple gestures are the most meaningful.
Don't start anything you aren't prepared to keep up!
Remember the old adage,
"The way to a man's heart is through his stomach."
Cards and flowers usually work.
Remember to say the words, "I love you,"
Remember that actions speak louder than words.
Treat each day as though it may be your last –
Have no regrets.
Keep friendship alive.
Make fun a priority.
Let laughter soothe your souls.
Be happy, healthy, and wise.
Learn from your mistakes and forgive freely.
Remember that hard times do come,
But they will pass eventually.
Remember the joy you are experiencing
this day, this moment.
This memory will sustain you.
Remember your promises before God and this company,
And that you never walk alone.

Dedicated to Heather-Michelle & Patrick 9/1/2000

MATRIMONIAL JOURNEY

Today you begin a journey of discovery.
You will discover that
You are not always right.
The toilet seat must stay down.
Flowers and cards score huge brownie points.
Praise goes a long way.

You will discover that
You have been truly blessed.
You have married your best friend,
Confidant, and loyal companion.
And most important,
You have in-laws that love you both!

You will discover that
Hard times will come,
but you will get through them together
However, you must remember –
You are a team.
Say, "I'm sorry."
Never go to bed angry.
Minds cannot be read.
Communication is essential.
Fight fair and forgive.

Remember the joy you are feeling today.
Remember the tears of joy shared
By family and friends this day.
Remember why you fell in love in the first place.
Buckle up and enjoy the ride!

Dedicated to Alexis & Leroy 4/19/03

Patricia Ann Woolfork

A FOUR LETTER WORD

What causes me to love you so?
Is it your crooked little smile
or your small shining eyes?
Do I love you for your tenderness, kindness,
And patience when I am intolerable?
Do I love you for your strength or
your fondness for good things?
What do I see in you?

I see a warm, bronze, beautiful soul
Whose embrace
would melt the largest mass of ice,
Whose kiss would shatter
even the most fragile piece of glass,
Whose touch makes my heart leap within.

Can these reasons be enough
or shall I enumerate further?
Alas,
There are not enough hours in a day –
Enough stationery to write upon
To explain,
To enhance upon,
To explore the breadth,
And the infinity of it all.
Be it enough
that these words express and say it best,
Darling . . .
I LOVE YOU!

TODAY IS A NEW DAY!

Today is a new day for both of us.
As your grandmother,
I am privileged to witness
The marriage of my first grandchild!!
Today is a new day for you because
You make your best friend your wife.
You are no longer roommates,
Boyfriend or girlfriend –
You are husband and wife!
Today you affirm what you have known
Since you were 13 years old . . .
"This is my soul mate!"

Today you are no longer playing house.
You are the husband – the man of the house!
This new role comes with responsibilities.
You must remember that neither of you are perfect.
You must love her as you love yourself –
Sometimes even more.
You must learn how to compromise,
Be patient, and to be forgiving.
You must remember what made you
Fall in love with her in the first place.
Keep doing what you did to get her – to keep her...
Keep romance alive even when the money is funny.

Have fun!
Make laughter a priority!
Love passionately and unconditionally!
Continue to make her feel special –
Build her up when she feels down.

Patricia Ann Woolfork

Tell her every day that you love her.
Kiss her "hello" and kiss her "good-bye."
Hold hands in public, and walk on the outside.
Open doors and be chivalrous – it is not dead!
Always control your anger –
Never,
Never,
Never be . . .
Physically,
Verbally, or
Emotionally abusive!!!

Do your best and be the best that you can be in everything.
Don't be so hard on yourself.
Expect difficulties, but remember that they will pass.
Remember that you have everything
Within yourself to be successful in all things.
Keep God in your life.
His Word will direct your steps!

Today is a new day –
The beginning of a new adventure.
Enjoy your new status . . .
Mr. and Mrs. Russell LaMont Simmons, Jr.
CONGRATULATIONS!!!

Love,
Nannu

Dedicated to my firstborn grandchild, Russell, Jr., on his wedding day, August 3, 2011

Day Dreams of My Soldier

As I sit here gazing aimlessly out of my window,
I see the littered walkways and slush
From yesterday's melted snow.
I can't help but wonder what the scenery must be over there
Where you are so very far away.

The mortars must be booming now
And the bullets never ceasing
And DEATH reaching up from beneath the earth
Carrying away its captives.
Men, women and little children
Running –
Searching –
Crying –
For a place to call home once again.
There is hatred all around you,
Yet you can still feel love for me
As you peer from behind a bunker trying to keep alive.

Can you remember how dreadful this dingy,
Slum-ridden town used to be when we were but children?
How we dreamed of an escape to faraway places?
Alas, some dreams should never have been dreamt at all.

Returning again to my window
I see small children playing –
Little boys chasing girls –
Filling the streets with childish merriment
Much the same as we used to do years ago.

Remember how foolish we were then?
Those were happy times.
I really miss our little spats and our goods days together
And the aspirations we shared.
I haven't given up hope
Because someday soon,

Patricia Ann Woolfork

You will return,
And we will pick up all the little pieces.
We will restore a relationship
That time and distance has hindered.
And we'll laugh . . .
And you will forget the sights you are now beholding . . .
And I will love you.

Dedicated to LSJ, Vietnam Conflict, 1969

I Should Have Told You

I should have told you how magnificent you look
With your salt and pepper hair,
Especially the way it glistens in your mustache
And frames your perfect mouth.

I should have told you why I avoided eye contact
Although I sneaked a peek every chance I got –
So afraid that I would again get lost
In the depth of that pool of gold in your eyes.

I should have told you
how great your arms felt around me,
How safe I felt lying next to you listening to you breathe;
And, yes, I watched you sleeping –
Longing to run my fingers through your hair.

I should have told you that I was afraid
Too disappointed in myself –
Too afraid that I was not enough for you
To take a chance to see
How far we could stretch our friendship.
Still too afraid
That you weren't over the chase for the younger girl.

I should have told you I found you sexy as hell,
And that I still get a thrill
at the sight of your leg in your tennis shorts.
I really wanted to watch you play tennis and cheer you on.

I should have told you I did want to make love with you,
But I was afraid that I wouldn't know
What my true motive was.
I wanted to be sure that it wasn't a desperate act –
One of simple longing.

I was afraid it would make me feel worse
For all the time I've lost not being loved or
Sharing my love with someone
Who meant something to me.

I should have told you how
Touched I was by your sentiment about our past.
I should have told you how
Pleased I am with the knowledge that
You'd miss me in your life in whatever capacity –
That I was "a thread in the fabric of your world."
(AWESOME!)

I should have told you so many things.
I should have told you
How much I want to be
Respected, cherished, and loved unconditionally.
I should have told you
I no longer want to settle to sit on the sideline
Watching what's left of life pass me by!

I should have told you how
Scared I am of being hurt or rejected, yet again.
I should have told you
I was afraid of letting my emotions get away from me.
They have been so out of control of late.
I should have told you
I held back because I knew I would be devastated
If I was truly a "booty call" –
Waiting another six years to hear from you.

I should have told you
I wanted to take a chance that my feelings
Were all unjustified,
But then again,
They are my feelings.

Savoring Eden

I should have told you
How much I enjoyed kissing you and
Hugging your warm, steamed body –
Smelling so good after your shower.
I should have
Undressed you and showered you with kisses.
I should have left you longing for more of me.
I should have left you spent and smiling.

If you know me like you say that you do,
Then you felt my ambivalence.
You saw my indecision.
You saw my lack of eye contact –
Have you ever seen that before?

Maybe we both should have
Just comforted each other
For all the loses in our lives –
Satisfied with the knowledge
That there are still a few people
That really care about us,
Secure in the familiarity
Of the years of our on again/off again
Tag – team relationship.

I should have told you
That I missed you long before
We said good-bye at the steps.
I started missing you
As we sat across from each other having dinner.

I should have told you how excited I was
At the possibility of seeing you again –
Sharing walks along the beach,
Going to concerts,
Listening to music,
Giving you breakfast in bed next time.
I should have told you
That I wanted to dance with you in the living room,

Patricia Ann Woolfork

Cuddle with you on the sun porch.
I should have told you
Everything!
I hope it's not too late
To tell you all that I should have told you
When I had the chance.

Dedicated to Vernon Clash, Esq.

WHAT I KNOW NOW

I know now
That you weren't really telling me the truth
About you wanting to be with me
Soul – mates of days gone by –
Finally ready to share our spotlight in time together.

I know now that my reading poetry to you was
Only a cheap turn on for you to jerk yourself off
While you lay in the darkness of your room
Turned on by the melody of my voice.

I know now that you were just being a man,
Telling me what you knew I'd love to hear,
Making me feel all warm and fuzzy
Thinking I was something special to you.

"Yes,
I am 'the thread in the fabric of your world'," you say,
But that fabric is quickly unraveling
With my unwillingness to be kept on stand-by
While you get your playmates in a row.

I was so caught up in the excitement
Of spending time with you
Watching sunsets,
Holding hands while walking in the sand,
Reading poetry while listening to the music you picked,
Remembering our youth
Sharing stories and music
Laughing –
You must have really had a good laugh
At how big a fool you thought I was.

I know that I come with baggage
Who doesn't?
I know that I am not fiscally sound,

But I do have my talents and my intellect
I can mix with the best of them.
I am not to be discounted because as you say,
"You need a job."
"You've got too much time on your hand."

I know now that you didn't mean it when you said
"I should have come and got you this weekend."
"I'll send you a train ticket by Thursday." –
Only to not hear a single word from you,
In what?
Nearly two weeks?

A holiday rolled by without a word.
A perfect opportunity to get together,
Don't you think?
Especially with someone you want
Not to disappoint this time?

I know now that I am too mature
To wait around like some teenager
Waiting for the phone to ring –
Waiting for the invitation to enter into your world –
Waiting to see if I fit into your plans –
Waiting to see if I am worthy of an audience with you!

I know now that I was wrong to consider
That you would be any different this time around.
You are good at your trade.
You maneuvered me around my defenses –
Opened me up for the let down
And dropped the ball right on my exposed vulnerability.

Yes, I should have told you what I felt.
I should have told you what I wanted in a relationship.
I should have told you
To go straight to hell with all your bullshit!

Savoring Eden

Maybe that explains my ambivalence . . .
My inner voice heard the sounds of bullshit brewing,
But my sense of longing for a connection
Muffled the sounds,
Turned off the warning bells
Left me deaf – disabled
With what might have been.

If by chance you find the time to grow up
And realize what a jewel is within your reach . . .
You'll stop playing games with yourself
Or with me.
Maybe it won't be too late,
But now that I know
What I know now . . .

(Dedicated to Vernon Clash, Esq.)

All romances have their ups and downs. He absolutely loved me chewing him out with this poem, almost as much as he loved the previous one. We've been friends since I was 12. We still are, only now we are living 1,000 miles apart.

Love Is

Trust
Warmth
Sincerity.
Without it one is void
Empty
Incomplete.
Love is the pinnacle,
The highest point one can attain.
Love is –
Life.

I Truly Hope So

The minutes ticked by slowly today
As I waited for you to walk by.
How I longed to get a glimpse
Of your smiling face and crystalline eyes.

You've remained in my thoughts since first we met.
I hardly remember our last conversation,
So mesmerized was I,
Lost in your soft gray eyes and dimpled cheeks.

I only know that I was spellbound in your presence,
Captivated by your friendliness,
Your candor,
Your charm,
And the sexiness of your voice.

Will we indeed meet again?
Share another moment in time?
Inhabit each other's space?
I truly hope so!

Passion: Hot & Spicy

LOVE DANCE

Hold me!
Kiss me!
Squeeze me!
Make me tingle all over!

Enfold me in your tender embrace.
Love me arduously.
Stroke me with lips, fingers, and tongue.
Heighten my ecstasy.
Renew my passion.
Restore my soul.

How I long to hear your heavy breathing,
Listen to your heartbeat,
Feel you tremble at my touch,
Feel the hardness in your trousers,
Bear your weight upon me,
Make you moan beneath me!

Sunrise Interlude

5:30 A.M.
Pale moonlight still adorns the sky.
The sheets are damp from the perspiration
      caused by my scorching body heat.
My respiration is labored, and
      my thighs are wet.
I longingly reach out for you, but
      you are not there next to me.
It was so vivid, so real . . .
      this dream of you and me.
So, I turn on the light, and
I fight the urge to call to see
      if you are awake,
      also bathing in an afterglow,
      having reached out for me
      only to find me gone.
I imagine that you are because . . .
      no dream should be that divine!
I could have sworn
      your arms were holding me close, and
      your chest hair was tickling my cheek.
I could feel the smile on my face and
The drumming . . . of our heartbeats.
I could have sworn
I heard you moan and call out my name.
I know that I felt . . .
      Your slow-moving,
      Earth-shaking,
      Lip-quivering,
      Soul-stirring lovemaking!
Did you feel my tongue?
Did you feel my hands?
Did you feel my breath?
Did you feel my lips on your face?
Did you feel me quiver and shake?
Did you hear my . . .

"Oh, my God!"
"Yes, baby, right there?"
Did you splash you face with water?
I sure as hell did!
6:45 A.M.
I am still too hot to sleep.
Hold that thought!

Dedicated to Dijait

Work Your Magic

I simply have to read your words on paper,
And I am instantly breathless.
My thighs become moist.
My desire mounts.
My body temperature soars.
My breasts rise and fall
With the rhythm meant only for lovemaking.

I feel you all around me –
Beside me,
Beneath me –
On top of me –
Inside of me.
You have no idea
How badly I want you at this moment.
My God!
I come with words on a page!
Will my heart survive the real thing?

I'm dizzy with desire.
Sweat has covered my brow.
My nerve endings are afire.
I fight my need to pick up the phone and
SCREAM your name!
Take me,
Take me, please!
Say something – anything
In that mellow tone of yours, and
I will become liquid at your feet.
Excite me as only you can.
My passion can no longer remain dormant.
You scare me with your intensity, but
I am too hot to care!
Work your magic all over my body.
Make me weak –
Take all my juice.

Savoring Eden

Mount me vigorously –
I like it like that.
Then, ever so slowly,
Make me cry the tears
Only good lovers know.
Take me to the edge –
Bring me back again.
Hold me
Like you have never held another.
Work your magic on me
Like your magic on the page!

Dedicated to Dijait

Patricia Ann Woolfork

FEELS SO GOOD

I've tossed and turned for hours.
My restless spirit moves my pen across the page.
I want to reach out and feel the warmth of you beside me,
But, alas, you are not here.
If only,
I could rest my head against your baby soft body,
Feel your arms enfold me . . .
What sweet messages would I relate to you?

I close my eyes envisioning you and I
Locked in each other's embrace
Moving to a love melody –
Our timing in sync –
Our heartbeats steady –
Our muscles taut.
Oooooh baby. Don't stop! Oh, that feels so good.

Rest your head gently upon my thighs.
Make me sing our song with your sweet tongue.
Make my breath catch in my throat.
Make my body melt to your touch.
Oooooh baby. Don't stop! Oh, that feels so good

Let me kiss you hungrily.
I want to consume your very soul.
Do you feel me quiver and shake?
Did you catch that purr?
Can you feel me inside of you?
I've invaded every cell,
You belong to me.
Every nerve, capillary,
Muscle, tendon, joint and bone
Responds to my love command!

Feels so good!
Can't stop . . .

Savoring Eden

Kissing your face, your neck, your belly button
Licking your ears, nipples, and chest . . .
I am wet in anticipation of our love dance.
Tease me, why don't you?
Tip in – tip out . . . Slow and steady and strong.
Let me drown you in my love nectar –
Squeeze you in my love grip!

Oooooh, baby. Don't stop!
Feels real good!
"Harder!"
"Break my back," I say.
"Hm, Hm, Hm," . . . You say
As you shiver, quake and moan
Probing for. . .
Untouched territory inside my body.
I become you and you become me –
Heart, mind, body, and spirit.

Hear that pop?
We are locked in a love ritual –
Licking, biting, pulling hair, clutching fingers,
Grabbing asses and headboards –
Sharing spit and sweat –
Stroking each other inside and out.
Oooooh baby. Don't stop!
FEELS SO GOOD!
Cum drips down my thighs,
                        Onto the bed sheets, and
                                      Into the crack of my ass.
Again, and, again, and, again.
Oooooh, baby. Don't stop!
SOUNDS real good, doesn't it?

Dedicated to Dijait

MEMORIES

I was moved by the poem
You read to me last night.
Had I really affected you that way?
Time has a way of passing quickly,
But memories are restored in an instant.

I remember you and me.
Our encounter was brief,
But vehement in its passion.

I remember how you moved me
With that poetic tongue of yours
And your potent virility.

I remember
The yellow rose,
The candlelight,
The music,
The friendship,
The late-night phone calls,
You missing me, and
Me missing you.

I was moved
By the poem
You read to me last night.
Thank you for the memories.

Dedicated to Dijait

RETROSPECT

I watch you sleeping so peacefully beside me,
Bronzed beauty that you are.
I remember last night –
Your lips searching hungrily for mine,
Your hands tenderly caressing my flesh.

I remember your desire awakening.
I remember your thumping heart,
As my nipples saluted your tongue.

I remember our passionate moans.
I remember how well we fit together –
Like hands in a glove.
Your body was made for mine.

I remember you holding me tightly –
As though you didn't want me to get away.
I remember feeling your love –
Despite your silence.

Do you remember?

WHAT?

What . . .
Do you see when you look into my eyes?
What . . .
Do you feel when my lips touch yours?
Do you feel my breath catch in anticipation?
What . . .
Thought crosses your mind . . .
When you touch me tenderly?

THE TWO OF US

Here we are
Two clean bodies
Embracing,
Touching, and
Loving.
Bursting with life and exuberance,
We find
Fulfillment,
Joy, and
Rapture
In one another's arms.
Everything surrounding us is beauty itself.
There is
Warmth,
Security,
Happiness and
Love engulfing us.
Silenced are the sounds of
War,
Death,
Disease and
Pain.
Only the sounds of love remain –
Only the two of us.

Dedicated to J. M. S. -- 5/20/75 1:30 P.M

THE PIANO MAN

Tickle me with those ivories, Rio.
Play that soulful melody as only you can.
Fascinate me with the syncopation of your keyboard.
Stimulate my senses.
Stir my heart with your expertise.

I travel to faraway places with each stroke of a key.
My toes are tapping to your beat.
My spirit cannot stay still,
So moved am I by the music you play.

Mesmerize me,
Hypnotize me,
Excite me,
Piano man.

Dedicated to the musical genius of Rio Clemente, 12/17/09

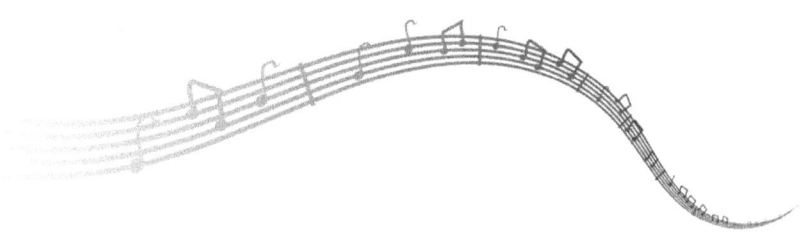

MR. BASS MAN

I watch your fingers
Lovingly caress your instrument,
And I hear the sweet melodies forth-coming
I think of you and me in each other's arms –
Fingers against flesh.
The sounds of our passion
Are full of soul-stirring rhythms.
I recall each stroke of longing
With each pluck of a string.
With each line you play,
I remember the music we played together.

Can you hear it?
Do you feel the vibe?
Do you remember –
The tune we played
With each other's secret places?

We are in perfect harmony.
Our timing is in sync.
Your up is my down.
Your down is my up.
Your song is my song.
Can we sing it again, please?

Dedicated to Michael Logan

Patricia Ann Woolfork

THE DENOUEMENT

I held you in my arms
And rocked you as gently
As a mom with newborn babe.
Swaddled in the warmth
Of my golden thighs,
I sheltered you from harm.
I kissed your face with a feather's touch
As you suckled my breast in earnest,
My sweet, beautiful, man child.

As I trace the smoothness of your skin
With the moisture of my tongue,
I feel your pounding heart
And hear your breath catch in your throat –
Caught in a passionate coo.

I feel your arms tighten their hold on me
Like a blanket in a baby's hand,
I know we have bonded soul and flesh
With the closeness of a mother and child –
Secure for the moment.
Armed in passion against the cold, cruel world outside,
We play tickle me games with fingers and toes.
We play body tag with expert skill.

Our bodies begin to quiver,
Like the wind in the autumn leaves,
We are bound . . .
By the cord of carnal knowledge.
My mind and body explode . . .
With that sense of knowing –
You may never be in love with me,
But –
You will never forget me!

The Budding Poet

Patricia Ann Woolfork

THE BUDDING POET

I add these pieces just to show how much I have, hopefully, progressed in my writing experience since the age of 15. The first piece was a homework assignment. My teacher thought it was cute, but she knew I could do better. She made me do a do over and bring it in the next day. That is the second poem in this section. From that point on, I challenged myself to write, but I was not really happy with rhyming.

I began writing again after my divorce from my childhood sweetheart, and this collection of poems is the result of my life's work. I hope you have enjoyed it so far.

JUST A LITTLE DITTY

(First poem ever written, Age 15, 1965)

Once upon a time
I had a little flea.
This little flea belonged only to me.
When we're at home,
He stays in my pocket;
When we're out on a date,
He's in my very best locket.

Out in the snow
Thirty degrees
Keeping him warm is merely a breeze.
Where the wind blows
Nobody knows,
But where ever I am,
My little flea goes.

This became a lullaby that I sang to my children and grandchildren when sick, sleepy, or cranky.

Patricia Ann Woolfork

MEMORIES AND DREAMS

Beneath the canopy of my bed
A soft, fluffy pillow to nestle my head.
When night has passed
And dawn creeps in
There's sure to have been a dream or ten.
From rags to riches, hate to love,
The earth, the sea, and the things above,
Enjoyed to the fullest, are the dreams of his love.

His love is like none other on earth
And I stop to wonder, "Of it am I worth?"
To dream of the times when he'd hold me tight
Oh, for the memory of his kiss good-night.
When he whispers sweet nothings into my ear
And cuddles me close and calls me "Dear."
Of the day he'll ask me to be only his,
My heart jumps for joy
It bubbles and fizzes.
For the times that I long for his touch
I know from the start, I'll enjoy it so much.
Amid his mass handsomeness, muscles and charm
As we stroll down the avenue
Arm in arm.

The many a days I peered into his eyes
Nothing to be compared to my surprise
To the day he said that he loved only me
What he dreamed that our lives together would be.

His eyes are hazel.
His hair is light brown.
He's built sort of nice,
(But how to describe him without using words twice?)

I know that I love him
He says he loves me.

Savoring Eden

If this be the truth, it will always be.
Not just one day, two, or three,
But our love will last 'til eternity.

Yes, my dreams do unfold events to behold
If they be true,
The color of blue will not be the color for me,
But I'll play the game right
And I'll stroll out in white,
As the bells cry "Ave Marie."

As we walk down the aisle to say, "I do,"
I'll be happy, but nervous
May cheeks will be blue
As we make of our hearts one heart,
We'll kneel at the altar making vows never to part.

I'll stick by him in thick and thin.
If I play my game good, I'm sure to win
When I turn around to look at Mom's tears,
I'll think for the moment of the years and years
We'll spend with each other "for better or worse,"
The rest that I'm thinking . . .
I can't write in verse!

When the minister says, "You may kiss the bride,"
What a moment of pleasure to be there by his side.
We'll raise a big family,
Maybe two, maybe three,
The best part of it all is,
They'll belong to him and me.

In time as we know,
Our children will grow
And there will only be memories,

But what a delight
To sit there one night
And think of the past histories.

Patricia Ann Woolfork

We'll have kept our vows right to the end
Once starting out to be only friends.
We'll have loved each other
"Through sickness and health."
To dream of his love
Is a great treasure of wealth.

Dedicated to LSJ, 1965 Age 15*

I married my high school sweetheart and we had three beautiful children, two sons and one daughter. Our "happy ever after" lasted approximately five years. We now have nine grandchildren, four boys and five girls, and one great-granddaughter.

STRONG

Strong mind.
Strong body.
Strong will.
Strong arms.
Strong man.
Strong woman.
Strong family.
Strong world.

Patricia Ann Woolfork

FROM ONE TO ANOTHER

They say that girls are made from sugar and spice
And everything nice,
But that's not entirely so.
And that little boys grow from frogs and toads,
But that's far from the truth as everyone knows.

Amid her curves and shapely lines
The female has her way
Strutting about with her nose in the air
Making the boys behave.

The two get together as everyone knows
And a new generation begins to grow.
They'll hear the same myths as their mother and dad,
For telling these stories are part of a fad.
But soon they will learn as they grow up like pines,
Leaving the tales they were told behind.

In come the new.
Out goes the old,
But nevertheless,
These same stories are told.

THE SWEET MEMORY OF LAVERNE

She hasn't just died
She's dead!
And yet I still can't believe
I can't get it through my head.

She was a good friend
A good friend, indeed
And personalities like hers
Is what the world needs.

When I think that
She won't look out of her lovely brown eyes,
It's as though a feeling of shock or sudden surprise
Comes over me.
It's sad, but true
That her struggle for life has all been in vain
Now, all that is left are her still remains

Why do some people affect me this way?
Christ! The only thing left for us all
Is to have faith in our Savior and pray.
It's strange that
We don't know a good thing until it is gone
And so others have died and the world goes on.

We'll miss you sweet child.
All the people you didn't know were your friends
Will do as I have and adopt you as kin.
Dearest LaVerne,
You'll be laid to rest in the cold dirt and clay
Perhaps awaiting the time
When God's words will come true about
"The Resurrection Day."

Patricia Ann Woolfork

Good-bye, good friend,
But it's only for now because
Someday,
Sometime,
Someplace,
Somehow,
God will wipe away all of this misery
And restore once again
The paradise
That was stolen from everybody.

Dedicated to my tenth-grade locker partner March 1965

A Change

The petals have fallen
The trees are bare.
Summer is gone.
Snow's in the air.
The birds have gone.
The wind is cold.
Animals sleep.
Men grow old.

The surf boards are in.
The toboggans are out.
The little white flakes are floating about.

The children play.
The snowmen smile.
The winter has come,
Over miles and miles . . .
The white carpet that glitters,
Is soiled by the shoes,
And sleigh rides are here again.
What wonderful news!

Patricia Ann Woolfork

SEARCH AND YOU'LL FIND

Where is happiness?
Do you find it everywhere?
What must be undertaken?
What hurtful schemes must one bear?

They say just grin and bear it,
The best is yet to come,
While feeling low and in despair,
What cheerful melody can you hum?

They say that happiness is just like gold –
Hard to get –
Hard to hold.
So learn to live and share
With people everywhere.
The things that must be done
Cannot be done by one.

With this one view in mind,
Only then will you find
HAPPINESS . . .
Is the answer to your prayer.

TRIANGLES

When the bonds of love are broken
Due to some outsider seeking to come in,
The sense of understanding
Once enjoyed by two
Becomes a triangular affair.

What exactly is the outside force
Which drives two lovers farther and farther apart
And cools the innermost emotions and passions
Once so abundant in their hearts?

Their love is like the unattainable pot of gold
At the end of the rainbow
After an April shower
And more beautiful
Than the innocence of Miranda and Ferdinand.
How indescribable was the imagery of this
Long-sought romance!

Should they give in
And allow such an intrusion
To cause such unhappiness?
Or, shall they become like Romeo and Juliet,
And extend their love to the gates of Hades
Where nothing can reach them?

Patricia Ann Woolfork

A GHOSTLY TALE

The moon is full.
The goblins are out.
The little black witches are flying about.
The cat's eyes glare.
The hooting owl stares.
The little people's feet
Are heard clomping up the stairs.

From door to door
And store to store
In masquerade, they parade
Their little hearts jumping with glee
As they think of the goodies which they will receive.

Yes, Halloween is the night,
The costumes can't be beat.
The night is right for any fright,
The kids say, "Trick or Treat?"

I Put My Baby to Bed

On Monday I put my baby to bed for the last time. It has taken years to get to that place where I thought she could be trusted to stay in for the night and not climb out and get into my bed again. It wasn't that she needed me in the middle of the night. It was me who could not do without her in my line of vision.

It felt just like when I first brought her home as a tiny infant—scared to leave her alone, always wanting to hold her in my arms until suddenly she was too spoiled to be laid down and had to be broken from the bad habit which I had caused.

She is out of the crib—out of the toddler bed—now in her beautiful queen size canopy bed. She is no longer an infant, but a full-fledged, beautiful young lady. I have fed her, nurtured her, encouraged her, prodded her, protected her, educated her, guided her, and taught her all that I know.

Today I had to let her go and let her begin to shine on her own, knowing I had given all I had to give. It is time to let her spread her wings, find her way in the world, and make a name for herself—without me. I have dressed her in her finest, polished up her vocabulary, dotted every "I" and crossed every "T" for her launch into independence. My baby is all grown up, a stunning trophy for a job well done. She is a tribute to my tenacity to never be complacent, strive for perfection, be thorough, and leave nothing out without becoming redundant.

In case you haven't caught on to this metaphor, I am talking about my manuscript of free-form poetry and prose which began when I was only fifteen years old—full of innocence, hopefulness, and naiveté of what lay before me in the grown-up world of love and living. I watched her leave that sense of "all is right with the world," and become awakened to the reality of betrayal, dishonesty, loss, depression, struggle, survival, and finally, transformation and victory.

So, today I finally put my baby to bed for the last time. I moved pages around, updated the *Table of Contents*, spell checked the Introduction and Conclusion, looked for omissions, made additions, put each part into a digital file to be forwarded to the publisher for layout, graphics, cover design, printing, and pricing. I added my final requests and recommendations and reluctantly pressed the send button.

Oh, it was as hard as I remembered my labor being almost fifty years ago—not knowing what to expect only fearing what *I* had been told about the pain—wanting to get to hold that baby that *I* had been carrying around for all those long, sick full, months. Finally getting to meet that little creature I had a hand in procreating was the most heart-warming, soul elevating, awesome and fear inspiring event in *my* life. And now I get to give birth again, but this time, way past the age of childbirth, full of expectation nonetheless—still having that gut-punched feeling of not having nearly enough knowledge about how to do it right, but also knowing my ability to overcome any obstacle, and endure with grace, is still a part of my wheel house.

Letting go is so hard for a Virgo. *But,* just like when you give birth to your child, the nurses and the doctor get to check it out, clean it up a bit, weigh and measure it, swathe it in a blanket and put a little cap on its head before they finally bring it over to you—so goes the process of writing to publication. I have faith that my baby will be given the best treatment, tenderly embraced in my absence, and presented to me cleaned and bathed, smelling baby fresh, and a beautiful reflection of her mother.

October 22, 2018

Conclusion

It has been my utmost desire to share my journey from childhood to adulthood of sexual, physical, emotional, and psychological abuse in an effort to help others understand that they are not alone in this most viscous assault to our childhood development. I say viscous because we never fully recover. It stays with us for the rest of our lives in bits and pieces, affecting all future relationships and our self-esteem.

We make huge mistakes that we later regret, but sometimes the damage to ourselves and others is often irreparable. Accepting ourselves as human beings with imperfections is the first step. Fully accepting that it was not our fault, we were children, leads us to a path of full recovery—no longer the victim.

Our testimony is important. It starts the healing process not only for us, but the multitudes of others with which we share our story. It does not matter how long it takes us to get our story out. It takes longer for others to come to grips with their trauma. Sometimes it takes the perpetrator's death to find peace. However, it is never fully over unless we address it, even if it takes years of counselling.

Losing our innocence and not knowing how to trust or have a proper relationship with others is the trademark of a childhood survivor. We feel unworthy and dirty and guilty, but that is far from the truth. We are a child of God first, and He loves us just the way we are. He puts people in our lives for various reasons—some to encourage us, and others to help us learn lessons so that we don't stay on the hamster wheel of life—going nowhere.

Some of us have chosen drugs, alcohol, promiscuity, abusive relationships, and co-dependency, ad nauseam, to get us from one day to the next—only to repeat a cycle of destructive behavior. Once we begin to discover our self-worth, we find other ways to build ourselves up and learn to love ourselves—something no other person can give us. That is why we continue to fail. We are enough. We are capable of accomplishing great things. Our past is not our destiny. We make it ourselves by what we do to change ourselves and the courses we choose to take.

I hope and pray that this book has helped you in some way, no matter how miniscule, to let you know that we all have value and purpose. We do and can make a difference. We are creative and resourceful no matter what someone tells us. We know ourselves better than anyone else.

To those of you who have read Savoring Eden for the artistic value that I hope you found, I am most grateful. I have put my heart and soul into observing and writing about the experiences we have with others that share our time and space on this planet, Earth. We are more alike than different. I hope you have seen yourself in my words, and have felt some of the same anxiety, joy, satisfaction, sadness, remorse, and beauty without having had the life of a survivor and found inspiration in them. Those are the things that make us brothers and sisters no matter the skin color, nationality, religious belief, societal status, income, or politics.

If I have brought you words to provoke thought, conversation, to find beauty when there seemed to be none, inspiration, reflection, understanding, and gratitude—then I have met my intended objective.

One last piece of advice: Celebrate Life. Be grateful. Love one another. Live in the moment. Be happy even in the bad times because they are only temporary setbacks. We all have enormous potential. Tap into it and find your state of joy and share it with others.

Sincerely,

Patricia "Trishann" Woolfork

Acknowledgments

The Huntsville Literary Association Poetry Workshop

John E. Carson's Creative Writing Class at the Huntsville Senior Center and Christine Brown and Anna Talyn Carson at CBA Publishing Services LLC

Newark, New Jersey Public Library

The Weequahic High School, Newark, NJ , English Department (Class of 1967): Mr. John. Silva, Ms. Helen Klayman and my mentors: Mrs. Janette Lappe' and My HS Guidance Counselor, Mrs. Weinstein who believed in me and pushed me toward higher education. My total gratitude for presenting my transcript to Kean College, Union, NJ, ten years after graduation, and securing me a scholarship and an on-campus job when I was a divorced, single parent with three young children ages 2-5. Weequahic was the home of famous author, Phillip Roth.

Kean University Speech/Theatre/Media and English Departments, the late Edith Wendt, PhD, the late Kenneth Larsen, PhD, Don and Gaye Lumsden, PhDs, the late James Murphy, PhD, to mention a few.

It took me five years to get my BA in Liberal Arts/Speech, Theatre, Media and Secondary English Education–Magna cum laude and Dean's List. I received my NJ Teacher of English Certificate K-12. I returned for post graduate studies and received my P-3 Certification in Early Childhood and 18 credits towards a master's degree where I remained on the Dean's List.

Mr. Bill Gouldd who started me on my Journey of Self-Awareness: Thanks for the trip. (Delmar, CA, 1990)

Kathy Russo, MSW, Reshma Patel, MSW, and Fleeta Bulle, MSW who took a "no holds barred" approach in helping me find my self-esteem: I could never tell you how much you helped me see the light. (Family Connections, Orange, NJ)

The staff at Rader Institute who showed me how to become a "survivor" and not a "victim": My undying gratitude! (April-May 1994) Des Plaines, IL

To my therapist Thomas J, Sandy, PsyD: my undying gratitude for your caring, uplifting spirit and generosity. He put the fire under me when I would bring in pieces I wrote to express what I was dealing with in this journey and urged me to become part of the Huntsville Literary Association to meet other artists and share my work and I got a piece published in their annual chat book. Thank you for all of your encouragement and pushing to get me to write again and share it with others. Thank you for believing in my talent and helping me with being able to use the voice I was not allowed to use throughout my childhood. Thanks for simply telling me to "Make It Happen." (2014-present)

My Best Friend, LaVonne Marie Adams-Hopkins: We have known each other since the third grade which means we were somewhere around eight years old, right? We have been best friends since the ninth grade which was somewhere in the vicinity of fourteen years old, right? We graduated from High School nearly 48 years ago, right? Too much information, huh?–(smile) I just want everyone to know just how long you and I have been real friends! A rare and valuable treasure! Thanks for sharing my tears and never holding my short-comings against me. Thank you for your unconditional love and for being my best cheerleader and critic. If there is a heaven, you'll be there one day. I love you.

*I lost my best friend, LaVonne, on November 25, 2014. My life will never be the same. I would like to thank LaVonne for listening to every word I ever wrote and believing in me and my potential without hesitation and unconditionally until the day she died. XOXOXO

Ditto To Dr. Carl Ross, MD: You have been in my corner for nearly thirty-eight years, as one of my oldest friends.

To the late Robert W. Potter, the late Edward "Butch" Caston, and the late Virginia Hughes: You are missed. Thank you for your unconditional acceptance, support, and love.

I want to thank a fellow poet named, "Dijait," who used to challenge me to answer his poems with one of mine. That is how *Hot & Spicy* started. I had been writing romance prose all along, but this pushed it up a notch.

I would like to acknowledge the late Jazz Deva, Rasheema Periera, formerly known as Gloria Smith. We met at one of her concerts. She liked my work and encouraged me to be her guest reader, and her band accompanied me. That experience is how "An Evening of Poetry & Jazz with Trishann and Friends" was created.

I would like to acknowledge the many musicians who played for me either at their own gigs, or at the gigs I would book for us together. We played at Jazz Festivals, Benefit Concerts, Jazz Clubs, Talent Shows, etc. Among them are: Gordon James, Radam Schwartz, Michael Logan, Bradford Hayes, Rio Clemente, Benny Barksdale, Jr., Cornell McGhee, Tomoko, and other New Jersey musicians.

And finally, I'd like to acknowledge the fans that followed me faithfully and bought over 240 copies of my first book, "Stop and Smell the Roses: A Poetic Journey into Relationships, Emotions, Nature, Sexuality, and The Development of Self Awareness" by "Trishann," (Patricia Woolfork-Simmons)

About the Author

Patricia Ann Woolfork (a/k/a "Trishann," the poet) a Newark, New Jersey native, graduated from Weequahic High School, home of the late Philip Roth, poet, David Shapiro, and Reese Schonfeld, et al, in the top 10% of her class, and received her BA Magna cum laude majoring in English, Speech/Theatre/Media and Secondary English Education and post-graduate Certification in Early Childhood Development PreK-3rd Grade also at Kean University.

As "Trishann", a pen name which she chose and her performance persona, she has written hundreds of poems, essays, and short stories. In the past she sold over 240 copies of a self-published collection of poetry. She has also been recently published in "Voyages: An Anthology" available on Amazon and cbapub.com.

She has read all over the United States at libraries, churches, cable television, a jazz festival, a cancer benefit, and booked events at Livingston Mall and area nightclubs as "An Evening of Poetry and Jazz with Trishann & Friends." She has been invited to perform at both weddings and funerals with her heartfelt, emotional portrayals of the human experience. She has also been published in several poetry anthologies and chat books.

"Trishann" (pronounced Trish–aunn) has long been recognized as the "sensual poet" because of her melodic voice and passionate renderings often accompanied by jazz. Her works cover the gamut of the human condition from birth to death, love, sexuality, relationships, joy, despair, and our commune with each other and Nature and Spirituality.

If perchance you know someone who has been traumatized as a child or an adult, whether male or female, the following book will help them understand themselves and help those that love them understand them as well. I urge you to get a copy.

"<u>The Courage to Heal: A Guide for Women Survivors of Child Sexual Abuse</u>" by Ellen Bass and Laura Davis. Third Ed., 1994 IBSN 0060950668, Harper Perennial, A Division of Harper Collins Publishers

Please feel free to send me feedback regarding your experience with "Savoring Eden," and how it may have affected you. I'd love to hear from you. I can be reached at:

author.patricia@cbapub.com

www.ingramcontent.com/pod-product-compliance
Lightning Source LLC
Chambersburg PA
CBHW051038160426
43193CB00010B/985